COMMUNITY LIBRARY

D0458687

The War at the Shore

Donald Trump, Steve Wynn,
and the Epic Battle to Save Atlantic City

Richard D. "Skip" Bronson

with Andrew Meisler and A. M. Silver

The Overlook Press
New York, NY

A special and heartfelt thanks to my assistant,
Pamela Brown, for her work on this project.

Copyright 2010, 2012 Richard D. Bronson

I've Been Everywhere, words and music by Geoff Mack,
Copyright © 1962 (Renewed) Belinda Music Australia Pty. Ltd.
All rights administered by Unichappell Music Inc.
All rights reserved. Used by Permission.

This edition distributed in the USA in 2012 by
The Overlook Press, Peter Mayer Publishers, Inc.
141 Wooster Street
New York, NY 10012
www.overlookpress.com
for information about special or bulk sales contact sales@overlookny.com

All rights reserved. No part of this book may be reproduced in any
manner without written permission of the publisher, except by a
reviewer who wishes to quote brief passages in connection with a review.
The scanning, uploading and distribution of this book via the Internet
or any other means without the permission of the publisher
is illegal and strictly prohibited.

Cataloging-in-Publication Data is available from the Library of Congress

ISBN 978-1-4683-0046-8

2 4 6 8 10 9 7 5 3 1

Book design: Mike Diehl
Type formatting by Bernard Schleifer Company

Printed in the United States of America

For Jeffrey Blau for always being there

Contents

Prologue

DONALD TRUMP'S HAIR IS REAL, and Steve Wynn sees better than you think. Much has been written about these men, but few people know them, personally and professionally, as well as I do. It's been said that to truly understand someone, you have to fight them or fight beside them, and I was at the white-hot center of a titanic clash of money and power that transformed Atlantic City from a struggling day-tripper place with buses in and out to a born-again destination drawing tourists from New York, Philadelphia, and other major cities along the eastern seaboard.

It's all quiet now on the eastern front of the American gaming industry: Atlantic City, New Jersey. But for five chaotic years, from 1995 to 2000, two of the world's best-known companies—run by two of our planet's most flamboyant businessmen—fought a bare-knuckled, high-stakes battle over a prime piece of real estate in one of America's most famous resort towns. No money was spared, no punch was pulled, no invective went unhurled in what became known as "The War at the Shore."

You may have read about this affair in the pages of *The New York Times, The Wall Street Journal, Time* or *Newsweek*. Or maybe you saw the segment about it that aired on the 1996 season premiere of *60 Minutes*. If you did, you probably think you know what happened when Mirage Resorts Inc. took on Trump Resorts Inc. for the right to be king of the hill in Atlantic City. You don't. You're not even close.

I was close. Very, very close. And after it was over, and despite my outward appearance of being an easygoing guy, the city's mayor described me as "the toughest mild-mannered man I know."

Steve Wynn, the founder and CEO of Mirage Resorts Inc., was my partner in this complicated saga. I was a member of the board of directors of Mirage and president of New City Development Company, the Mirage subsidiary whose primary purpose was to build a top-level new casino and hotel complex in Atlantic City.

Steve Wynn was—and still is—a genius entrepreneur, an unbelievably hard-working and dynamite-tempered perfectionist whose imagination and chutzpah have transformed Las Vegas and the entire gaming industry throughout the world. Book smart as well as street smart, a man frequently described as having partial blindness, yet incredible vision, Steve Wynn picked up in Las Vegas where Howard Hughes left off. He has reached heights even Hughes couldn't have imagined.

Donald Trump was—and of course always will be—the brilliant New York-based real estate mogul, airline industry dabbler, reality TV star, and tireless self-promoter. Back then, they were battling over who would be king of the hill in the biggest sandbox on the East Coast. The outcome, to put it mildly, was still very much in doubt.

As for me, Richard "Skip" Bronson, I am a complicated All-American success story: a product of a fractured family and city-owned housing project in Hartford, Connecticut. A former paperboy, spelling bee champion yet college dropout, and prolific developer of shopping centers and office buildings—including

CityPlace, Connecticut's tallest skyscraper. Steve Wynn entrusted me to create an environment in which he could bring his brand of beyond-belief projects to completion.

I had worked with Steve for several years when the idea of his returning to Atlantic City surfaced. The man who had established the new standard for resorts in Las Vegas with his pioneering hotel-casino the Mirage had a plan to bring the same level of entertainment experience to New Jersey. Donald was operating three struggling hotel-casinos in A.C., so the prospect of our arrival on "his" turf was as appealing to him as zero-karat gold in Trump Tower. In other words, he would do everything he could to stop us.

And I mean *everything.*

The War at the Shore

CHAPTER ONE

Chasing the Prize

THERE WAS ONLY ONE DAY when I was truly afraid for my life. It was an unseasonably muggy New Jersey evening, the kind of night when sunset did little to relieve the heat. I had come down to Atlantic City from my home in Connecticut with the purpose of convincing the local residents—people I didn't know and knew little about—that my company's proposed hotel-casino would rescue their neighborhood from the decay that had consumed it. With me I carried the promise of jobs, thousands of jobs that would revitalize an economy screaming for opportunities. But my message of hope bore a caveat. In order to go through with the project, several homes would need to be razed; a few people would be inconvenienced, so that many more could afford to put food on their tables and send their kids to college. The numbers were on my side, but arguments aren't won with statistics and battles aren't fought on paper.

I was talking about a casino, a building where they could work, a tool that would bring in revenue for their government; they were talking about their homes, the roofs under which they put their children to bed, the places where they took refuge from the demons and drudgeries of the world. A home is sacred, it's not just a plot of land; it's the cornerstone of the American Dream, and as far as the folks in the 6th Ward of Atlantic City were concerned, I was the man who was going to take that away from them.

I entered a dingy room lit with insipid fluorescent lights that gave the 200 or so people packed in next to each other a sickly look. Cracked walls, littered with graffiti, shed paint on an un-swept floor. I walked up to the microphone, which was attached to a speaker the size of a toaster oven and several years out of relevance, and introduced myself to the crowd.

"My name is Skip Bronson, I'm from Mirage Resorts." I went on to explain that we would build a complex in the vein of the colossal Las Vegas palaces, not just another tinpot collection of slot machines like the venues that ran up and down the Boardwalk. Our hotel-casino would employ 5,000 people right off the bat, and this didn't mean just croupiers. It also meant housekeepers and valets and waiters. I assured the congregants, "You will not be disqualified for lacking experience."

"What, are you saying we're stupid?" a man in the crowd called out.

"No, not at all. I just want to assure those of you that haven't worked in a casino that prior experience is not a prerequisite. We will provide jobs for you and train you to do them."

An overweight man in suspenders with a scraggly beard bellowed, "You don't care about us. All you care about is tearing down our houses so the white man can get more money."

I was the only white person in the room and my expensive suit was in sharp contrast to the jeans and T-shirts worn by the men and women I was speaking to. However, I never considered myself part of the establishment. I was a Jewish kid from a poor neighborhood in Connecticut. I grew up sharing a room with my sister and had worked in some capacity for as far back as I could remember. I knew what hardship was like, and I knew it was something that could be escaped.

"This casino is a chance for you to change your lives. It's going to benefit your community."

My claims were met with choleric stares and loud boos. The low ceilings felt as if they were coming down on me. I have always had the ability to find the right words at the right time, but this was a situation where there was no right answer. I wanted to say, "Look around you. Look at the conditions you're living in. Don't you want to improve them? Don't you want something more for your children?" But I couldn't. They took umbrage to any disparaging remark made about their neighborhood.

I tried my best to restate my proposal, but it was to no avail. A woman in the crowd cried out, "We don't believe anything you have to say." At that point, I should have left. I should have turned around and headed right out the door. There was no way to get through to the crowd; but I stubbornly clung to the belief that if they would just let their emotions subside, they'd see my logic.

I had no such luck. The epithets kept building, and they weren't just about the casino. I was getting blamed for things that had nothing to do with me, such as flooding in their homes. These people had been mistreated for a long time and there was a knot of anger that had been festering for years. This meeting was their outlet for all the complaints that had gone unaired. The politicians who had abused them weren't there; but I was. They were an angry mob with torches lit, and they saw me as Frankenstein's monster. I was getting yelled at from all sides and as the feet shuffled and the noise heightened I felt nervous in a way I never had before. Out of the corner of my eye, thankfully, I saw a black policeman in full uniform, his gun clearly displayed. He was a big man; he didn't seem intimidated, and I thought: At least there's one person here who's dedicated to keeping the peace. A few minutes later the officer marched up to the microphone to make an announcement. The crowd parted to make way for him. We were all ears.

"Before they put a brick in front of my house, I will throw a brick at them!" he shouted. By "they" and "them," I realized, my heart thumping, he meant *me.*

———

When I was fifteen-years-old and earning a few bucks—thanks to a bogus license—driving cars for the nightly auto auction, I had no idea that I'd eventually find myself in the middle of one of the most hotly contested real estate battles this country has ever seen. I had handled my share of professional adversity and knew the kind of political maneuvers that are the true foundations of our most impressive works of architecture, but the struggle over Atlantic City was the defining event of my professional life.

It didn't begin in the governor's mansion or the Mirage Resorts' Las Vegas headquarters. The genesis didn't lie in some Boardwalk casino cage or one of the many palaces that make up the Trump Empire. No, my journey started on that verdant variation on the corporate boardroom: a golf course.

———

In the 1970s, I used the first "real" money I had made in real estate development to buy a condo at the famous La Costa Hotel & Resort in Carlsbad, California. I spent as much time there as I could playing a lot of golf and hanging out. It was the perfect place to escape the brutal Connecticut winters. One day, Irwin Molasky, one of the resort's owners, told me he had a good friend coming over who'd just taken up golf and Irwin wanted me to play a round with him.

I said, "Irwin, please don't make me play with someone who's just taken up the game. How about if I have a drink with him?"

He said, "No, no. I want you to spend time with him. His name is Steve Wynn."

I paused. "Steve Wynn, as in the Golden Nugget Hotel Steve Wynn?" At the time, the Golden Nugget was one of *the* hotel-casinos in Las Vegas. Wynn was the wunderkind of the gaming industry.

I thought it would be fun to meet him, so I figured why not? Little did I realize that my decision on that day in 1983 would mark the beginning of a personal odyssey that continues to the present.

———

Steve Wynn looked like he could have easily belonged on Wall Street or K Street, but he had set his sights on Las Vegas instead. Trim and well dressed, he walked with a visible confidence and emanated an enthusiasm that pulled in all of those around him. Some men have a way of making every word riveting, and when Steve spoke in his exuberant baritone, you felt as if there was thought put into every syllable. He was then forty-one years old, I was thirty-eight. True, he was a beginning golfer but it was obvious he was athletic. Clearly he'd researched the subject, and he was determined to make up for lost time. A congenital condition called retinitis pigmentosa was affecting his vision and limiting his depth perception on the course. But his intensity and eagerness—make that compulsion—to learn more and get better quickly was remarkable.

There was something else. Steve Wynn had something special about him: an aura, charisma. After only eighteen holes I knew he and I were a good match. Some men are blessed with ideas, some men have the financing to support the ideas of others, and some men have the ability to see such long and arduous endeavors through. A strong businessman might even have two of these qualities. Steve was that rare individual who possessed all three.

———

You don't need an MBA to become a successful real estate developer. Even if you have one from Harvard or Dartmouth or the University of Phoenix, there's no guarantee you'll ever break ground on Project One. To make it in my business you need the right personality; the innate talent to convey your ideas to other people quickly and clearly; a knack for assembling close-knit teams of people with wildly different skills and eccentricities; the flexibility to stop, think, and make a major mid-course correction in the middle of several other major mid-course corrections; and, most important of all, a passion for working insanely hard and accomplishing ridiculously ambitious goals against overwhelming odds. You don't pick up any of these traits in a classroom, from a textbook or at the knee of a Nobel Prize-winning economist. You have to be born with a sense for the game, and you have to continue to hone your skills while managing the many obstacles that inevitably come your way.

A good developer also has to have a great imagination and an eye for seeing possibilities. For example: where you might see a few blocks of decent-enough looking office buildings or apartments, I might see the buildings knocked down and a profitable shopping center built in their place. Where you might have a favorite shopping mall, I know *why* it's your favorite shopping mall—why the subtle mix of location, anchor stores, and traffic flow make you reach for your wallet with a smile.

They say you have to walk before you can run. Well, I was such a hyperactive kid that I couldn't wait to get a move on and ended up skipping before I had mastered basic ambulation. My father called me "Skip" and it's the name I've been going by ever since. Born in Hartford, I started my business career in the mailroom and later, writing news copy at WTIC. The Travelers owned the radio station, and it wasn't long before I turned from journalism to selling insurance.

There are very few lifers in the life insurance business—it can be a depressing and onerous job—and I was not one of them. Though I was doing well for my young family, I saw much brighter possibilities in selling homes rather than just knocking on doors. So I decided to give development a shot and it turned out, I had a gift for real estate. Developing in Hartford was an old man's game, but I ascended the ranks quickly. I restored my one-time father-in-law's ailing real estate business, and at the age of 33, earned the nickname "The Boy Wonder." I took satisfaction in seeing my work shape my native city's skyline; and before I reached the age of 40, I had achieved more than my parents could have ever hoped for. But in 1991, banks throughout Connecticut, including my two primary banks, went under, and out of desperation, called in all their unsecure loans. My partner's misjudgments forced me to file Chapter 7 bankruptcy and brought down the company I had worked so hard to build.

After my company disappeared along with most of my money, my biggest fear was that I, too, would disappear. I went from the best office suite in Hartford to working out of a tiny office off my bedroom at home. Looking back, the most valuable asset I possessed was the urgent certainty that I had to reinvent myself—and *fast*.

———

What I saw in Hartford in 1992 was urban blight—and opportunity. On its way to becoming a hollowed-out wreck of a city, Hartford had no industry to speak of besides insurance. Its tax base was pitiful. As a tourist or convention destination it ranked somewhere around Hoboken, New Jersey, or Topeka, Kansas.

On the other hand, something fascinating was happening in another economically troubled area of Connecticut. In the far eastern corner of the state, which was hit hard by cutbacks in the defense industry, the Mashantucket Pequots were building the first casino west of Atlantic City and east of Las Vegas. The thought occurred to me in my little office: why not fight for legalized gaming in Hartford? I'd seen the money and jobs it had created in Las Vegas and seen how people such as Steve Wynn—especially Steve Wynn—had been able to turn godforsaken patches of desert into entertainment and tourism Meccas.

After our golf match at La Costa, Steve Wynn and I had kept in touch. A few years later I was in Las Vegas for an International Council of Shopping Centers (ICSC) convention. I decided to give him a call, wondering if he'd remember me.

His secretary, Joyce Luman, answered and asked me to hold on. Within thirty seconds Steve was on the phone. He asked where I was calling from. I told him I was at the Las Vegas Hilton.

"Pack up your bags," he said.

"What?" I said.

"Pack up your bags. There'll be a car to pick you up downstairs. You're not going to stay there. You're going to stay over here at the Golden Nugget."

I said, "Well, the meetings I have are actually all at the convention center, and it's more convenient to stay here, but how about if we get together for dinner?"

Steve wouldn't hear of it; he'd make sure that there was a limousine on standby for me 24/7.

When I got to the Golden Nugget, which Steve had reinvented after taking on a majority interest in 1973, I was escorted to a massive suite on the top floor. It was the biggest hotel room I had ever seen. In fact it was more like a glamorous apartment. I had done my fair share of business travel and had become inured to even the finest hotels. But the suite at the Golden Nugget was something else: two stories with windows stretching floor to ceiling, a spacious living room, an elegant dining room and all of it done with exquisite taste. It was more spectacular than the Presidential Suite at the Waldorf-Astoria, the kind of room your friends had to check out for themselves because otherwise they wouldn't believe you.

That night Steve and I had dinner together, and we had a blast. Even in the midst of our eating and shooting the breeze I was blown away again by his passion and breadth of knowledge. My experience with casino executives was that they were excellent at marketing and promotions, but Steve was more than that, he was a true developer. If he had wanted to do shopping centers, his malls would be where you went to shop. If he had wanted to build condominiums, we'd be lining up to live in them.

To ascend to that level requires not only remarkable talent, but also an unrivaled attention to detail. I had the pleasure of playing the first round of golf at Mirage's private Shadow Creek golf course along with Steve, famed shopping developer Melvin Simon, and Steve's biggest casino customer, high roller Ken Mizuno. How important was Ken Mizuno to Las Vegas? Well, in the changing room at Shadow Creek, Steve Wynn had locker number two. Though the four of us stepped out onto a course in the middle of the desert, we felt as if we were in North Carolina. Surrounding us were 10,000 trees, each with a sprinkler to help it survive the inhospitable conditions of the Mojave. It was an incredible sight, but Steve felt there was something amiss. At the base of the pine trees, there weren't any needles accumulating as they usually do. Now most people would let this pass. Not Steve. He went down to Arizona, had some trucks load up on pine needles and drive up to Nevada, just so the needles could be sprinkled around the course. That's the kind of perfectionism he brings to everything he does, all in the pursuit of, "creating a place that will make people say, 'wow.'"

———

By the early 1990s Steve already was well known as the man who had reinvented Las Vegas as much as, if not more than, other famous moguls such as Howard Hughes and Kirk Kerkorian. His Mirage Hotel was the first Strip establishment where gaming was only a part of the total entertainment package.

These days, it's easy to take for granted the preeminence of the Strip in Las Vegas. The Wynn, Venetian, Bellagio, Mandalay Bay and other mega-resorts dominate the landscape and the economy. But not too long ago, Las Vegas Blvd. was known for now demolished casinos built in the 50s such as the Dunes, the Sands and Desert Inn. The city was split between downtown and the Strip. The Mirage tilted the battle. It became the epicenter of Las Vegas and ushered in a new era of development and a new philosophy in design.

Steve and I had discussed several projects before, but a casino in Hartford was a whole other ballgame. It wouldn't just change my native state; it would reshape gaming across the country.

I called Steve and said, "This is a long shot—but did you know that the Indians are about to open a casino in Connecticut?"

"Yeah, I heard about that," he said.

"Well, I was talking to the Senate majority leader in Connecticut. We're very friendly, we grew up together, and he and I think that there could be a chance that we could convince the government of Connecticut to allow a casino as an urban revitalization tool. Not just a gambling place, but the kind of thing that you do that's very unique. Something like what you did at the Mirage."

He said, "Really, Skip? You really think that they might go for something like that in the Land of Steady Habits?"

I said, "I really do."

Not exactly an ironclad guarantee, but Steve seemed intrigued. Though he hadn't spent much time in Connecticut, Steve was a native of New Haven. At this point his daughter was going to Yale, and he said, "You know what? The next time I come back to visit Gillian, I'll take a ride up to Hartford and you can show me around."

"Fine," I said, and at that precise moment my reinvention program began.

CHAPTER 2

Code Red

THESE DAYS there are casinos everywhere from Detroit to Mississippi, but in the early '90s, gaming was basically confined to Nevada and Atlantic City. When Steve wanted to build a casino in Las Vegas, there was no need to wage a campaign. The politicians wanted to be helpful in promoting new developments and did all they could to aid their most talented businessmen. Connecticut would be the first time Steve encountered serious opposition from the local government. However, he was willing to give it a try.

If you took five steps back and looked at it logically, nothing made more sense in 1992 than authorizing casino gaming in Hartford. The city was on its ass financially and there were no new industries on the horizon. The resort that Steve Wynn wanted to design, fund and build there would create more than 8,000 new jobs, most of them for unskilled workers. The tax revenue would be a tremendous boon and the buzz would rejuvenate the city. Hartford was perfectly located at the intersection of two interstate highways: two hours by car from New York City *and* from Boston *and* from Providence, Rhode Island. With Atlantic City still rinky-dink and Las Vegas a long plane ride away, all anyone would have to do was open the doors and visitors from all over the Northeast would flock to the revitalized city.

There are those who find gambling to be immoral, but there are many more who find it less distasteful than taxes. If there's a choice between alienating a few constituents or alienating all of them, most politicians will stifle their prejudices and go for the casino, and the truth is that most states now allow gaming. It's called the lottery. When the states introduced the lotto, they basically gave up the theoretical weight behind their objections to gambling.

Connecticut had had a state lottery since 1971, followed by off-track betting parlors, pari-mutuel betting at dog tracks and jai lai frontons seemingly since the French & Indian War. Not only was the environment right for a Mirage casino, but having one was the next logical step for the city.

Besides, Connecticut already *had* full-fledged casino gaming in the Mashantucket Pequots' Foxwoods Resort Casino. Well, almost full-fledged gaming. There was one very important exception: no slot machines. Slot machines at Foxwoods would have been the casino's biggest moneymakers, as they are for many casinos; but at the time, they were illegal in Connecticut. Actually, the only reason table gaming was allowed was because they were sometimes used in other capacities. For example, charity events often featured blackjack tables. Well, that made it okay for the Pequots to put blackjack tables at Foxwoods. But slot machines were absolutely outlawed.

Since the Indians' reservation was considered a sovereign nation, none of its gaming revenue went to the state of Connecticut. By contrast, any agreement the state would make with Mirage and New City Development undoubtedly would include a hefty percentage of the profits—hundreds of millions of dollars per year—that would go straight into state and then city coffers. Sounds like a slam dunk, eh?

———

Not exactly. There was a basic reason why Hartford never seemed to be able to get out of its own way, a reason I confess that, even as a native Hartfordian, I didn't fully understand at the time. There was a civic mindset, smug and self-satisfied, that the way things had been done in the past was exactly the way things should be done in the present and in the future. Part of that was respect for the town's history and traditions, but a bigger part was fear of change and of outsiders—and worse, fear that these same out-siders would have better ideas for Hartford and/or criticize it for the backwater that it had become.

Detroit has the automotive industry, Los Angeles has film and television, and, of course, Hartford was known as the hub of the insurance industry. Companies such as Aetna, Connecticut General and Travelers still pretty much ran things. Why would they want another power player in town? During the course of our long fight, the Hartford insurance moguls proved stubborn opponents, lobbying against us and donating to anti-gaming legislators. In hindsight, they should have been worrying more about their own imminent extinction than about the actions of Mirage Resorts.

The Mashantucket Pequots, flush with millions of dollars in new gaming profits and eager to keep their monopoly in the state, threw their resources against us. The leader of both the Mashantucket Pequots and the tribe's long, hard fight for financial inde-pendence was Richard "Skip" Hayward—what are the odds of a Jew and an Indian whose paths would soon cross having the same first name and nickname?—but their fight against Mirage was led not by Skip Hayward, nor anyone even resembling a Native American, but by a lawyer named G. Michael "Mickey" Brown. Mickey Brown was the CEO of the Foxwoods casino operation in Ledyard. A native of northern New Jersey, he was a public prosecutor who made his name by convicting Mafia soldiers in that state. Then he ran the New Jersey Gaming Commission, where he set up niggling rules and regulations that eventually convinced Steve Wynn to sell his successful Atlantic City Golden Nugget. Brown made a great living for a few years as an international casino-industry consultant before being hired by the Pequots. He was smart and tough. Not a good opponent to have.

The Hartford Courant also lined up against Mirage and New City as did the mayor of Hartford, Carrie Saxon Perry. Of all the people involved in Mirage's campaign for casino gaming in my home state, the strongest and most important was governor Lowell P. Weicker, Jr. A smart and eccentric, even enigmatic, guy, Weicker had a substantial role in forcing Richard Nixon to resign during Watergate. He was from an old-line WASP family, the son of a Stamford-born business executive who had been the CEO of Squibb, the pharmaceutical company, and Bigelow Carpet. Weicker was raised in luxury in Manhattan and Long Island, and when the time came he graduated from prep school and then on to Yale and the University of Virginia Law School. He spent a few years as an officer in the Army, made a half-hearted effort at earning a living in the private sector, and in 1962 ran for the Connecticut state legislature as a Republican from Greenwich, a town as wealthy as Hartford was poor. Republican candidates always win in Greenwich.

From there it was on to the U.S. House of Representatives and three terms as the liberal Republican senator from Connecticut. In 1988, he was narrowly defeated by then-Democrat Joe Lieberman and fell out of favor with the state Republican Party. In a surprising 1990 comeback, he ran for governor as an Independent—the nominee of something called The Connecticut Party—and, amazingly, won. One big problem, though: in order to beat the Republican candidate, who promised no new taxes, Weicker had to promise not to raise taxes, either. After his inauguration, faced with a nasty recession and a big budget gap, he had to backtrack and ram a tax raise through the legislature.

After that bruising turnaround, Weicker welcomed any diversion he could find and any moral "high ground" he could occupy. He found his cause by opposing legalized gaming. He had fought bitterly against the Mashantucket Pequots' push for gambling in Connecticut because the Pequots were of little or no help to him in his budget battle. Almost everyone we met who was in favor of the project—and this included majority and minority leaders—urged that Steve meet with the governor and try to garner his support.

The two powerful men were a study in contrasts: Steve dressed neatly in his expensive custom-fitted suit and Weicker in that shambling-but-actually-expensive striped-shirt-and-suspenders look that rich WASPs like. Still, Wynn and Weicker seemed to get along beautifully. It was a low-pressure meeting; just a "meet and greet." They talked about art and art history, common interests, and it looked to me like a friendship might be forming. They were both Ivy Leaguers and had a passion for education. Weicker seemed caught off guard to learn that the Mirage actually had classrooms where employees could get a G.E.D. Steve knew all about Weicker and was intrigued by the governor's role in Watergate.

A few hours later we sent State Senator Billy DiBella over to the governor's office to sound out how the meeting had gone from that end. Billy DiBella and I had been friends since we were teenagers. I first met him when, cruising around in my 1952 Chevy convertible, I picked up his sister Andrea—we were stopped alongside each other at a traffic light. After literally chasing me out of his family house, Billy realized I was a pretty good guy.

Of course, that was some time back. Now William A. DiBella was a savvy Democratic legislator and Majority Leader of the Connecticut State Senate. From the silver sheen of his cotton candy coif down to his spit-shined shoes, he was polished. He'd even managed to clean up his language, well at least when he was addressing the Senate. Just as country singer Mel Tillis lost his stutter when he sang, Billy was able to switch off his compulsive swearing when in session. His colleagues might be surprised to learn that in general conversation, Billy would often interject some derivative of "fuck" the way a Valley girl would pepper her sentences with "like."

After checking in with the governor's office, Billy came back to us with good news. "Yeah, Weicker liked Steve," Billy said. "He was very fucking surprised by who he was. He didn't think he'd be that fucking refined—he'd expected a typical 'casino guy' but realized when they met that Steve was an extremely literate and articulate man."

About two weeks after that, we set up another meeting with Weicker. This would be the one where the subject of casino gaming would actually come up. For a series of complicated political reasons, we were told, this discussion should not under any circumstances take place "under the capitol dome," as the saying went. Nor should it take place in private. This should be an out-of-the-office-but-still-in-public kind of a thing; somewhat like a "just for fun" golf date with a client where you'd bring up the next big deal right after he hits a seeing-eye approach shot that stops five feet from the pin.

After some negotiation, both sides agreed that we would get together at a local haunt called the Hearthstone, which was the restaurant of choice for all out-of-town politicians and lobby-ists. If we were seen with the governor there—and we definitely would—it would be fine because it was a place where Weicker had lunch a lot, and whatever we were talking about with him couldn't be a bad thing because we were talking about it with him in the middle of everyone else who might be interested. And of course, everyone who *was* interested knew exactly what we were talking about: bringing casino gaming to Hartford.

After we all sat down and ordered lunch, Billy DiBella, fol-lowing protocol exactly, said: "Governor, this is no secret. I've been having conversations with Skip, my lifelong friend, and Steve Wynn, my new friend, about how they could do something to infuse some real excitement and enthusiasm into Hartford."

"I'm interested," said the Governor. "Tell me more about it."

Steve said, "I can basically do three things. I can employ an awful lot of people, draw one heck of a crowd, and pay a lot of taxes."

Weicker said, "Amplify that. What do you mean?"

Steve said, "Well, we think that we could create eight thousand new jobs here in the city of Hartford. And for every new job we create, there will be two new indirect jobs in the community."

Wynn and Weicker couldn't have hit it off any better. It was a case of: "Here, try my chicken." "No, no. You have to try my steak." They were literally eating off each other's plates.

True, Weicker never came right out and said, "Yes, I'd like to see a casino and entertainment complex" —but he didn't say no, either. We took that as tacit approval; that the governor was fine with it. Weicker was not one to stick his wet finger into the wind. If he was against you, he would tell you right out. He would point that finger in your face and say, "Let me tell you something. Not on my watch." If he were out to get you, he wouldn't stab you in the back; he'd stab you in the chest. That's the kind of guy he was. So when he didn't say "no," we thought, he was really saying "yes."

———

People have asked me, "What's it like to work with Steve Wynn?" There's no short answer because the man is so multi-faceted. He's not always easy to deal with, but he can afford to be exacting, because he's usually right.

Sportscaster Jim Gray invited Steve and me to go to the 1995 Masters Golf Tournament in Augusta, Georgia. Never having been to the Holy Grail of golf, this was sure to be a special experience for me. To top it off we went to the championship along with a mutual friend, basketball superstar Julius ("Dr. J.") Erving. When we arrived on Friday night we learned that Jim had made arrangements for us to watch the tournament from the broadcast tower between the fifteenth green and the sixteenth tee. Unfortunately, this incredible vantage point went to waste because of Steve's somewhat limited peripheral vision. He couldn't fully appreciate what was going on.

Gray suggested that we watch the last round from the broadcast truck where Frank Chirkinian, the ayatollah of golf broadcasting, was directing his thirty-fifth Masters tournament. As we entered the truck I saw a bank of television monitors, maybe forty in all, against a wall. We sat down behind Chirkinian and his assistants, next to the shadow of a figure sitting on a bench in a darkened area in the back of the truck. Knowing that I would be sitting next to this person for quite some time, I introduced myself.

I stuck my hand out and said, "Hi. I'm Skip Bronson." The gentleman sitting there stuck his hand back and said, "Hi. Mickey Mantle." Are you kidding me? Mickey Mantle! For a sports fanatic like me, this was practically an out-of-body experience.

It was extraordinary to sit there and watch the Masters unfold right in front of us, from the moment the theme music came up and the broadcast began. It was a lot easier for Steve, too, because he could easily shift his gaze from monitor to monitor and follow the action.

Frank Chirkinian growled into his microphone, "OK. Camera Two, we're coming to you next." At that point, Steve said, "No, no. Camera Five has a better angle."

I could see the hair on the back of Chirkinian's neck rise. He literally bristled.

Chirkinian's next call was, "Camera Seven, tighten up a little. We're coming to you." Steve said, "Have him pull back. Show the azaleas. Sell the magic."

This time, the director issued a low growl. Then Chirkinian said, "Camera Seventeen, get a tight shot of Tom Kite." Steve said, "No, no. Kite's not your story."

With that Frank Chirkinian yelled: "THERE'S ONLY ROOM IN THIS TRUCK FOR ONE FUCKING DIRECTOR!"

Steve slouched back onto the bench. He didn't say another word for the rest of the telecast—until the end when he noticed that announcer Jim Nantz's tie was crooked and told Chirkinian to have Nantz adjust it before the green jacket ceremony. "Nantz, straighten your tie," Chirkinian barked.

When the theme music came up and the broadcast ended, all the production staff in the truck high-fived each other to celebrate another successful Masters telecast.

Frank Chirkinian came out of the truck, walked over to where I was standing, and tapped me on the shoulder.

"I don't know how you put up with it," he said, "but I have to admit…he had a couple of great ideas."

As far as Mirage Resorts Inc. was concerned, Steve Wynn was Frank Chirkinian, Mickey Mantle, Tom Kite and Hootie Johnson (for atheists, the undisputed high priest of the Masters Tournament) combined. Mirage was a twenty thousand-person organization, but all niceties about corporate governance and boards of directors aside, many believed it to be a one-man company.

It was Steve's genius to treat his rank-and-file employees superbly—the croupiers, waiters, pit bosses, and housekeepers—the idea being that they would turn around and treat the hotels' guests superbly in return. It worked. To that end, Mirage's salaries and benefits were the best in the industry; in his obsessive drive to follow through, Steve even made sure that the employees' cafeterias —in most hotels a fluorescent-lit back room with folding chairs and metal tables—were as nicely decorated and had just as good a menu and service as the guest restaurants up front. In fact the company was honored one year by Fortune Magazine as the #2 Best Employer in the U.S.—ranked behind only Coca-Cola.

However, in the executive ranks things were not quite so cozy. Steve is undeniably a tough taskmaster. In the highest reaches of Mirage, some people made it their business to avoid Steve's attention entirely. Among others, there was a constant competition to grab precious minutes of Steve's time to suggest new and innovative ideas (good) or let him know of alleged screw-ups made by their rivals in the company (bad). And when Steve got angry, he really got angry.

———

My Connecticut lobbyist, Patrick Sullivan, told me that it was important that Steve and I meet with the legislature's black caucus and get their support. Patrick said, "Just sit down and listen to them. They're going to ask you for everything under the sun, but you don't have to deliver anything, all you need to do is quietly hear them out. It's all about respect."

Steve happened to be in New York at his tailor. I called him up and said, "Steve, it's crucial that we meet with the black caucus. We need their support if we're going to get this thing off the ground. Now Patrick warned me that they're going to make a lot of demands, but we just have to listen to them, we don't have to say 'yes.' Okay?"

He agreed and hopped on a plane dressed in his newly altered royal blue suit. The meeting started out cordially with introductory small talk, then, as expected, Marie Kirkley-Bey, the head of the black caucus, told us what Mirage had to do to get her support: "We need a new senior center, a new community center, a new urgent care center…" and on and on. It seemed as if all we had to do to build a casino was construct an entire town around it.

I thought back to Patrick's advice that we just sit there and listen, but I could see Steve was having a hard time keeping his emotions in check. I was afraid steam might literally come out of his collar. It reached a point where he just couldn't hold it in any longer. He stood up, indignation written all over his face, and declared, "Lady, you obviously have me confused with Santa Claus. He's the guy that wears the *red* suit!" and with that, the man in the royal blue suit stormed out of the meeting and flew back to Las Vegas.

The next day he called me up and casually asked, "So how bad is the fallout?"

From his tone I could tell he didn't think it was that bad. It was. "You only set us back about three months," I replied.

"Seriously?"

"Seriously."

"Well how do we fix this?" he asked.

"Well, if we want Kirkley-Bey's support, we're going to have to go over to her house and make amends. The sooner the better."

A lot of people find it easier to say "Oh, well" than "I'm sorry," but the next week Steve flew back to Connecticut, we picked up dinner and headed over to Kirkley-Bey's house, where Steve somehow charmed her back into our camp. I thought to myself: "Man, he can make bridges out of ashes."

———

It looked like our proposal was in really good shape. Not quite. Governor Weicker, using the first of several thunderbolts he'd reserved, let me know that ultimately he was *not* going to allow us to build a casino in Hartford. Not in person, of course. He let me know through Billy DiBella.

One summer day Billy reached me at my office in Las Vegas and said, "I've got fucking bad news."

"What bad news?" I said.

"Weicker does not want a fucking casino in Hartford."

"What?" I said.

"Yep," said Billy.

"You're kidding me!" I said. "We're already ramped up and we're rolling here."

"No," said Billy. "He doesn't want it. He's fucking saying that this is the capital city, he's got insurance companies to deal with here, it's not gonna be a popular thing, and Hartford's going to be fine without gambling."

Billy added that Weicker had his own ideas how to re-energize his capital city, plus—and this was a very big plus—he was getting a lot of pressure from certain "city leaders." I had a feeling I knew who those were. The insurance companies didn't publicly come out against us. They didn't have to. They controlled the city's economy and were able to use people like Tim Moynihan, head of the Greater Hartford Chamber of Commerce, to voice their dissent.

Then Billy delivered the "good" news.

"However," he said, "Weicker told me he would not stop this from happening in Bridgeport."

My first reaction was not positive. "Bridgeport?" I said. "*Bridgeport?* That's the worst. It's a disgusting place!"

Which it was. And still is, sad to say. But when Steve and I and the members of my team really talked about it and thought it through, the city of Bridgeport—about sixty miles southwest of Hartford—didn't look all that terrible. Connecticut's most populous city, it was an hour closer to New York City and all the potential customers we could attract from there.

We got a tour of the city from Mayor Joseph Ganim. He was a short, personable man who wouldn't disagree with you, well, not to your face. There isn't a lot of power that came along with being the mayor of a city like Bridgeport, but he didn't miss an opportunity to flex his relative muscle. It didn't matter if the streets were empty, he'd still employ the flashing red light that signaled a city official was out and about. It didn't matter if there was an available metered spot, he'd park in an illegal space. Why? Because he could.

Ganim showed us around his pitiful city. It was urban blight personified, one of the worst looking places I'd ever seen in my life. Although Bridgeport was only an hour's drive from Hartford, I had rarely ventured off the Connecticut turnpike onto its streets, and for good reason. Simply stated, it was one of the saddest American cities anyone had ever seen. It made Hartford look like Beverly Hills. In a strange way, though, this was good news for us—because the city was so desperate it would take any lifeline thrown its way.

After our visit I spoke to Billy DiBella about repositioning Mirage's effort for a casino in Bridgeport. He said there was no way we would ever get a deal approved in Bridgeport without including the definitive big fish in that small pond, a local power broker named Bob Zeff. He owned the dog track in Bridgeport and had been a major political contributor over the years. Billy said that although Zeff wasn't powerful enough to get approval to build a casino there on his own, he definitely had enough thump to stop us. Also, because he was the city's only person in the gaming business, he could pressure the local politicians not to allow us to build a casino unless we located it at his dog track.

Steve certainly wasn't happy when he heard the news, but he agreed to go to the track to meet with Zeff. The Bridgeport dog track, known as the Shoreline Star, was built around 1970 and it looked like the last money ever spent on the place was probably in 1971.

Robert Zeff was a sly-looking character: late fifties, rail thin, always dressed in a bulletproof dark blue suit. At least it looked bulletproof—it was certainly shiny enough. Zeff was a very successful personal-injury attorney, originally from Detroit, who somehow wound up owning the Bridgeport dog track. Behind his back we called him the "Prince of Darkness" because of his somber demeanor. Zeff was a very wealthy man, but you'd never know it by looking at his surroundings. I've seen janitor's closets that were better decorated than his office. Still, Zeff considered himself a full-fledged gaming mogul, and resented Steve Wynn for getting all of the attention whenever he came to town. Steve, on the other hand, resented the fact that we had to partner up with someone he perceived to be a third-rate guy. It was a match made in hell.

The day we announced the casino proposal for Bridgeport we held a press conference at the dog track. It had been agreed that I would be the master of ceremonies, and that Zeff would introduce Steve Wynn *briefly* and that Steve would make the presentation. Zeff promptly got up and prattled on for twenty minutes. Steve fumed. Sitting on the dais between Zeff and Steve was like being stranded in a demilitarized zone. More than once Steve leaned over to me and said, "Get him off!"

It's safe to say that, among the two hundred local politicians and reporters from Connecticut and New York City in the audience, no one besides Zeff's wife Suzie was there to hear Zeff articulate his vision. Finally, Steve couldn't take it any longer. He reached up onto the podium, grabbed a wooden pointer—it looked like the type a schoolteacher would use—and proceeded to whack Zeff behind the knees to remind him to wrap it up before sundown. It was all I could do to keep from falling off my chair in hysterics. Fortunately, Zeff got the not-too-subtle message and sat down. Then, as expected, Steve had the audience in the palm of his hand.

———

Flashbulb memories—those times in your life when something inside tells you that this moment is a pivotal event and your mind instantly captures not only the circumstances, but also the feelings in exquisite detail. On the morning of January 13, 1993, I was in my car, headed west on State Route 4 to an obscure radio station in Torrington, Connecticut, for a live on-air interview. The phone in my car rang. It was Patrick Sullivan.

"Oh my God, Skip!" he said. "Turn the car around! You've got to come back! We've got a Code Red!"

Code Red? "What's going on?"

"Weicker just held a press conference. He announced a deal with the Mashantucket Pequots to allow them to have slot machines in exchange for a lot of money!"

It got worse. Much worse. For allowing the Indians to install the machines in their Ledyard casino, Weicker had extracted from the Mashantuckets a binding agreement, the first of its kind with any state, to pay Connecticut 25% of their slot winnings. But here was the real killer: the agreement also stipulated that the Pequots wouldn't have to pay the state another penny if and when any other casino gaming company—that meant us—was ever allowed to operate slot machines in Connecticut. And oh, yes: the compact was expected to bring in about a hundred million the first year.

The cunning Weicker also decided that he wasn't going to stick this windfall into the state's general fund. What he did was even smarter: he doled out that money to each city in the state based upon its population. Basically, each city in the state could now help balance its budget with Mashantucket money; thereby cutting Mirage off at the knees in every municipality in Connecticut. Apparently, Weicker and his chief of staff, A. Searle Field, had been negotiating secretly with Mickey Brown for months (after leaving the government, Field started a consulting firm. His biggest client? Foxwoods). The historic Mashantucket slot machine deal was signed, sealed and delivered with absolutely no input from the state legislature, the public, or anyone else.

Foxwoods is currently the largest, most profitable casino in the world, a distinction it never would've garnered without slots, and the slots were a direct result of Mirage's efforts to build a casino.

———

I have absolutely no recollection of driving back to Hartford after hearing the news. What I do recall, very distinctly, is taking Steve Wynn's first phone call on that awful day. Bad news travels fast, and it came immediately after I hung up with Sullivan.

"Shut it down!" Steve said. "SHUT! IT DOWN! WE'RE OUTTA' THERE!"

It was the first, but by no means the last time I heard him say those exact words. He always used them when angrily declaring he was going to pull the plug on one of our projects. I did what I usually did in those situations: stall.

"Steve! Wait a second," I said during a very brief pause. "This thing just happened. It's still bouncing around like a ping-pong ball. I literally haven't yet turned the car around. Let me go back to town and find out what's really going on." Eventually, after a few more minutes of venting, he saw the benefits of not doing anything for the next few hours and agreed to wait for my analysis of our situation.

What I discovered back in Hartford seemed to justify my judgment. I quickly learned from Sullivan and my team members that most of the members of the Connecticut State Legislature—who had learned of the Mashantucket slot machine agreement the same time everybody else in the world had—were furious with Weicker. Here they'd been methodically plodding through all the issues involved with legalizing non-Indian casino gaming in their state—doing what their constituents elected them to do—when Governor Bigfoot had settled this all-important question without even consulting them.

Even worse—although from my side, even better—it was well known that Weicker absolutely despised most of the politicians he'd high-handedly ignored. The Connecticut legislature met only part-time; most of the senators and state representatives held down other jobs, and not just as lawyers, either. There were bartenders and railroad conductors and telephone operators as well. In Weicker's eyes these men and women were far below his level—and he never passed up the chance to let them know it.

When we talked to the Connecticut legislators we found that many of them wanted revenge—and in the most appropriate way possible. True, there still was a hardcore minority against gaming for moral or religious purposes, but many of the formerly undecided members now informally pledged their support to Mirage. We counted our potential votes many times and decided that achieving the two-thirds majority needed to override the governor's veto was possible. Close, but possible. We would keep fighting.

——

May 24, 1993, was the day our casino bill was scheduled for its final vote in the Connecticut legislature. May 24 was a Monday. The Friday before that, May 21, I got a call from Patrick Sullivan. "The Speaker of the House and Mary Fritz [the House sponsor of the bill] want to meet with you," he said. I went to meet with them in a conference room in the Capitol. Another incredible situation was unfolding.

Tom Ritter, the Speaker of the House, had trouble looking me in the eye. "Listen, Skip, what you've accomplished is incredible," he said. "But the bill isn't going to run. We're not gonna put it to a vote."

"What do you mean?" I said. "We've counted and think we've got the votes to beat Weicker's veto. Isn't that what we've been working on for all these months?"

"We don't feel certain we have the votes for a veto-proof margin," Ritter added. "And we don't want to take it to a vote."

I said, "Well, *we* want to take this to a vote, because we spent all this time, all this money. *We want to put this to a vote!*"

Mary Fritz and Tom Ritter then explained the facts of legislative life to me. "If we were sure it was gonna pass, that would be one thing," said the Speaker. "But to ask politicians to go way out into to the middle of the road and stick their necks out to vote for something that opponents can use against them in their next election—uh-uh. We won't do that."

The reason, they explained to me as if I didn't know, is that gambling is a highly controversial issue. It's often treated like the death penalty or abortion—a real hot button. And if our bill was going to fall short of the two-thirds majority needed to override Weicker's certain veto, which they had a feeling it would, they didn't want to make a lot of politicians record a vote that was going to offend their church and offend their constituents, leaving them hung out to dry on the wrong side of an issue that wasn't going to pass anyway.

CHAPTER 3

Take a Hike

I HUDDLED with Sullivan. "So we're screwed? Just like that?" I said. He shook his head and said, "Not completely." He told me there was something else the two legislative leaders wanted to tell me.

Patrick said that Weicker would be out of office the following year (he decided not to run for re-election and subsequently became a board member at World Wrestling Entertainment), and the likely Republican candidate for governor in 1994 would be a thirty-six-year-old guy who had impressed nearly everyone and was definitely pro-casino. In fact, he had publicly stated his support for it.

John Rowland had started out in the Connecticut state government and had made it to the U.S. House of Representatives before he was out of his 20s. Now he was aiming to be the youngest governor in Connecticut history. Politics suited him well. He was a real backslapper, literally, and made good use of his frat boy charm. Like Bill Clinton, Rowland had a habit of picking out the one person in a room that didn't like him, and instead of avoiding this individual, Rowland would walk right up to him and win him over. Slick and charismatic, he backed up his swagger with a quick intellect. He could give you an answer before you had finished asking your question. If you had to pick a leader out of a lineup, he's the guy you'd choose. He was a natural.

In 1994 Rowland promised me straight out that when he was elected, a Mirage resort, complete with casino gaming, could open in the Nutmeg State ASAP. He'd have to invite competitive bidding from other casino companies, he said, but he was confident we could all handle *that* situation. The main point was the Mashantucket Pequots would have no role whatsoever in the bidding. As much as we did on the up and up to get Rowland elected, the Indians did even more to support his anti-casino opponent.

In the middle of the campaign I got a call from the candidate himself. "Hey, Skip!" Rowland said. "It's squeeze time here, because there's a guy who's going to throw us a very expensive fundraiser at his home. And I need a celebrity. A big name. And as long as Steve Wynn is so tied into all those celebrities in Las Vegas, I need you to get me a big-name celebrity to attend the event."

Steve dug into his inexhaustible supply of celebrity friends and managed to get Bruce Willis, a staunch Republican but a guy who'd never met John Rowland in his life, to come to Connecticut for the evening. A helicopter flew Willis to Hartford from New York City, where he was filming a movie. After a couple of hours of glad-handing a bunch of starry-eyed strangers, the *Die Hard* star choppered back to Manhattan. The evening was a major success and somehow I convinced my future wife Edie, who's a passionate liberal Democrat, to dance with lifelong Republican Rowland for the good of the cause. She still reminds me of this occasionally.

I first met Edie Baskin when Steve and I were asked to meet with the people from *Saturday Night Live* about the idea of an

SNL Café at the Mirage. I had no idea who she was. Didn't know she was the *Saturday Night Live* photographer from day one (who took all the great photos of John Belushi, Gilda Radner, etc.). Didn't know she was from the Baskin-Robbins family. What I did know was she was stunning. I *certainly* didn't know that one day we'd be married.

———

In November 1994, John Rowland squeaked past William Curry by three percentage points. Both state houses got Republican majorities, turning Billy DiBella from the Majority Leader into the Minority Leader. New City Development "dusted off" plans to build a casino in Bridgeport, as Hilary Waldman so kindly wrote in the *Courant*.

First, of course, we had to prove to the legislators that our non-Indian casino could replace the revenue lost when the Mashan-tuckets, under the terms of the Weicker compact, stopped paying their hundred million a year. No problem. We estimated that our place would bring in at least one hundred and sixty million dollars for the state. But what about the gap between the time our casino was approved and when it was open for business? No problem. Marc Schorr, Steve's right-hand guy who was responsible for opening the company's new projects, said we'd build a giant temporary casino, practically overnight, and keep money for the state treasury rolling in. Competition from the other casino companies? With our local roots and knowledge, and our years of preparation, we had an advantage on all the other bidders, which included Harrah's, Bally's, Circus Circus and Trump Hotels. Piece of cake.

———

I had first met Donald Trump about 25 years earlier. At the time, he was a kid that made a lot of noise, but who nobody really paid much attention to. Now, he came to Connecticut as a rock star, perhaps America's top business celebrity with a social life chronicled in the tabloids and the most talked about hairdo this side of Don King. The people of Connecticut were all set to be mesmerized by him.

Edie and I spent an enjoyable afternoon watching Donald make a presentation to a group of Connecticut politicians at the state legislative office building. His slide show was a non-stop display of—well, Donald.

"Here's my personal 727 jet." Click. "Here's Trump Tower." Click. "Here's my office in Trump Tower." Click. "Here's my house in Florida, Mar-a-lago." Click. After twenty minutes of this I could tell that Trump had completely blown his chances with these people, many of whom held down blue-collar jobs to make a living. Of course, getting a casino in Connecticut wasn't Donald's aim. He was just covering his bases while his lobbyists tried to protect his Atlantic City interests by protesting gambling up north. I had no idea at the time that Trump and Mirage would soon be going head-to-head in New Jersey.

———

In early 1994 I had an idea how to turn our enemies into allies. Under conditions of strict secrecy—but always keeping our "friend" in Bridgeport, dog track owner Bob Zeff, informed—I reached out to the Mashantucket Pequots in hopes of recruiting them as our partners in a new Connecticut casino. I thought that if they saw the fantastic things Mirage had done in Las Vegas they'd figure it was to their advantage to associate with us. Besides, Steve and I were getting tired of battling with them. If we joined forces we would be up and running in no time. There would be more than enough money to go around. We figured a casino that close to New York could gross close to two billion dollars a year.

We invited all the tribal leaders out to Las Vegas and put them up in the best accommodations we had. I distinctly remember that tribal president Skip Hayward, for some reason, brought a large part of his American coin collection with him and showed it off to everyone during a reception. Steve and Elaine Wynn and Edie and I were there, and we duly marveled over the coins he'd taken out of their elaborate carrying cases.

During that weekend we made our pitch for joining forces. The Indians went away looking happy, saying they'd consider our idea. I called my friend, Kevin Tubridy, who was working for the Indians, to find out how our offer was going down. He called back and told me that the Pequots were very much taken with what they'd seen; that they didn't make decisions quickly but would convene their tribal council to talk it over. I was content to wait them out, see what decision they'd come to, then try to make a deal.

Not quite as patient as we were, Bob Zeff went behind our back to try to cut his own deal with the Indians. I never found out exactly what he proposed to them, but his secret plans apparently didn't include us. I learned about this from Patrick Sullivan—during the weekend of my wedding to Edie, no less.

In the middle of the wedding festivities, I phoned Zeff from the Mirage, furious beyond measure, and cut him a new one in language too strong to repeat. But the damage had been done. We never heard back from the Indians about our proposal.

———

On July 24, 1995, Mickey Brown submitted a letter to the state announcing that the Mashantucket Pequots were making a complete one-eighty and *would* be bidding on a casino in Bridgeport. On August 4, John Rowland used his gubernatorial powers to reopen the entire bidding process, issuing a "Request for Proposals" that imposed harsh financial terms, including a $610 million bond that each gaming entity had to post before it was eligible to bid (the purpose of the bond was to cover the fact that the Indians would no longer have to pay for their monopoly). Rowland arrived at $610 figure by calculating a loss of $122 for five years (though it would've taken us a little more than half that time to be up and running). I was beyond flabbergasted.

I went to David O'Leary, who then was the governor's chief of staff, and said: "What are you doing? What are you talking about? Why this new RFP? We invented the idea; we funded this whole thing. We're the ones that have been here for years doing this thing—now all of a sudden you're gonna go out and request proposals? And from the group that has been the main opposition?"

O'Leary said, "Oh no, Skip. Don't worry. We have to do this so that it doesn't look like this was a fix, that we just handed you the keys to this casino opportunity. We've got to at least go through the process of making sure that it's open and fair. It's just something we have to do. But it's obviously gonna wind up with you. Mirage is the company everyone wants."

It didn't smell all that obvious to me. I waylaid the governor at a charity golf tournament we were both playing in at a course in Farmington, Connecticut. I wasn't in his foursome, but at one point we crossed the same fairway in our golf carts, Rowland going in one direction and me going the opposite way. He saw me motioning to him and stopped his cart next to mine.

I said, "Governor, what's the big idea with this RFP? You want to bring the Indians into the process when the Indians are the ones that have been putting up all these millions of dollars to stop this from happening? And you want to invite them to make a proposal? Why?"

Rowland looked me straight in the eye, smiled, and said, "Nothing to worry about, Skiparoo!" He gave me a big wink and drove away.

A little while later, still reeling, I ran into Jodi Rell, Rowland's lieutenant governor (and ultimately his successor), at a reception in the clubhouse. I knew her fairly well. "Jodi, what's going on here?" I asked. "I just saw the governor and he said, 'Nothing to worry about, Skiparoo,' but what is the strategy here? Just so I'll know. I'm totally befuddled by this."

Ms. Rell patted me on the shoulder and said condescendingly, "You know, Skip, the governor is a very bright guy, he knows what he's doing, and you're going to turn out fine."

At the September 6 deadline only two bids for a Bridgeport casino were submitted—one by Mirage and the other by the Mashantucket Pequots. We obtained the required $610 million letter of credit. The Pequots didn't, but—surprise!—the special committee ruled that this didn't eliminate them from the competition. Their argument was that the Pequots were already paying the state so the Indians could be given a pass; this was all very well and nice, but the RFP specifically stated that the credit applied to all bidders and the absent letter should have eliminated the Pequots from the bidding process. The governor announced he would assemble a three-person panel, headed by Frank Muska, a professor at Western Connecticut State University, to evaluate the bids and recommend which one should be submitted to the legislature for approval.

I got the word through our lobbyists after a few weeks that

Muska was definitely leaning in our direction. Then I got a phone call from David O'Leary inviting me to an informal chat at the Capitol.

We met in the governor's anteroom. He started off by asking me the strangest question I'd ever heard in my life. "This casino thing," he asked. "Are you serious about pursuing this?"

Am I serious about pursuing this? I couldn't believe my ears. It would be like me asking O'Leary: "Would you like to live for the rest of the day?"

It was so absurd that I didn't even give him an answer. I said, "You didn't call me over here to ask me this. I mean, we've spent millions of dollars and I've spent several years of my life trying to get this done. What are you really saying?"

He started to hem and haw. "Well, this whole thing is very controversial…the Indians are paying all this money…it's probably going to be better for everybody…there might be a way…"

"What are you saying? What's the point?" I asked.

He said, "There might be a way that we could get you reimbursed for some of the money your company has spent on this."

"How would you do that?"

"Well, you know. We'll go and we'll tell the Indians that we're gonna sort of make you go away, but in order for you to go away, you've got to be paid something."

Why would we let anyone pay us to go away? We were going to win. Frank Muska's committee was going to recommend us. We had the votes in the legislature. The governor had told me I had nothing to worry about. We had the Triple Crown. I terminated our Alice-in-Wonderland conversation, and went back to work.

———

Then came the dagger. At 10:15 a.m. on October 2, 1995, Connecticut Governor John G. Rowland held a news conference and announced that he had selected the Mashantucket Pequot Indian tribe as the preferred developer of a casino in Bridgeport. He would call a special session of the state legislature that same month to consider only their proposal. Mirage's proposal, he said, was pretty good but inferior in several respects to the Indians', which would "continue to provide much-needed funding for our distressed cities and towns." There was no mention at all of the Muska committee or its recommendation, whatever it was.

I still don't know exactly what happened to derail Mirage's bid, and I'm not going to make any accusations. However, knowing what I now know about Rowland, let's just say that if something inappropriate occurred during the bidding process, I wouldn't exactly faint dead from disbelief.

Back in 1995 I wasn't quite as cynical. As soon as the decision was announced I gathered all of Mirage's biggest legislative supporters together in a meeting permeated with pure outrage. The object was to voice our indignation and signal our intention to protest Rowland's insupportable actions with the hope we could force him to re-evaluate his position. We chose an especially ticked off delegate to meet with Rowland and let him know how mad we were. The guy's name was Chris DiPino, a hopping-mad and seasoned Republican state representative whose other job was as a conductor on the Metro North railroad. If anyone could accurately represent our indignation, it was Chris DiPino.

DiPino met with Rowland the next day, assuming he would get this injustice reversed. Then...silence. I tried to get DiPino on the phone, but for some reason he wasn't taking calls from me or from anyone else in the pro-Mirage camp. A few days later the disappearing man reappeared at Governor Rowland's side.

Together they announced the name of the new chairman of the Connecticut Republican Party: Chris DiPino.

At this point I decided it was finally time for Mirage to fold its tent. But before we packed up I went to some of the legislators I'd befriended. I said, "You know what went down and you know how I feel about it."

I didn't need to say anything more. They assured me that they wouldn't let Rowland get away with it. A week later, there was a vote in the Legislature and Governor Rowland's enthusiastic call for a Foxwoods casino in Bridgeport failed. It was the first major setback of his governorship.

———

After the casino battle ended, my hometown, Hartford, fell into an even deeper recession than before. The reason was that the local insurance moguls, who thought they'd be in power forever and fought so hard to keep their headquarters city pure as the driven snow, began disappearing one by one. In 1996 Sandy Weill, the CEO of Citicorp, decided to buy The Travelers of Hartford. But Weill lived in New York, not Hartford. CNA, from Philadelphia, bought Connecticut General and became Cigna. Aetna was bought by U.S. Healthcare, which interestingly enough is also from Philadelphia.

The insurance industry isn't completely gone from Hartford; but all those towers downtown were suddenly branch offices, not headquarters. Just a huge group of file cabinets. That meant a loss of thousands and thousands of back office and insurance industry support jobs.

It also meant that people such as Sandy Weill don't care much about the Hartford Symphony or the Wadsworth Atheneum. When the big-shot CEOs were living in Hartford they were all passionate about supporting the local arts, but now the first thing you say if you're an out-of-town insurance tycoon looking at your annual budget is: "What's this million dollars a year we're giving to the Hartford Symphony?" Then you draw a big line through that item—because there's nobody around to remind you, "No, no, no. That's *our* symphony."

———

The reason Las Vegas is America's fastest-growing city is because of all the new jobs created by the casino industry. Meanwhile, Connecticut continues to lose population each year. Hartford is a murder capital and Bridgeport continues to be one of the most impoverished cities in the U.S. I don't have nearly as much sympathy for the people who worked so hard to keep Mirage and/or non-Indian casino gaming out of Connecticut. A few years later I ran into the highest-ranking staff member of the Greater Hartford Chamber of Commerce. The Chamber, taking its marching orders directly from the insurance industry, fought tooth and nail against us.

I said, "Gee, it's a good thing we didn't get casino gaming in Hartford. The insurance companies might have left." He blanched dead white and turned away.

In 1997 Mickey Brown was removed as the Pequots' CEO by a tribal faction hostile to Skip Hayward. Hayward was removed as tribal president by the same group the following year.

Joe Ganim, the five-term mayor of Bridgeport, was convicted in March 2003 on sixteen counts of racketeering, conspiracy, extortion, mail fraud, bribery, and filing false income tax returns. He was sentenced to nine years in federal prison.

As for former governor John G. Rowland, you've probably read about how much of his administration was corrupt: especially how his contractor pal William A. Tomasso (whose company built the Farmington golf course where Rowland told me that I had "Nothing to worry about, Skiparoo!") did free work on Rowland's house in exchange for no-bid state contracts worth millions of dollars. There was a lot of other funny business, some involving a now-defunct Texas company called Enron, but Rowland cut a plea deal with the feds that included him spending a year and a day in jail. He got out on February 12, 2006, but remained under house arrest. These days you can listen to him on his radio talk show.

By far the weirdest fallout from the whole affair involved Bob Zeff and Frank Muska. Zeff was furious that the Mashantuckets had been chosen and Muska was angry that the recommendation of his committee had been completely ignored. These two unlikeliest of friends bonded, and together they devised a strategy to uncover exactly what had motivated Governor Rowland to jump the fence on us and support the Indians' proposal.

Lo and behold, Zeff decided to take Frank Muska on a fact-finding mission to Las Vegas. Don't ask why he took Muska there, or why Muska ever agreed to go, but it was obvious that Rowland had the police keeping an eye on Muska because he was worried that the spurned professor was going to do something that would embarrass the governor. Investigators greeted Muska and Zeff at the airport when they returned from Las Vegas, and later found that Zeff had paid all of the expenses. As a result, Muska was discredited, and the governor announced that he was going to be appropriately punished.

Zeff also was in Governor Rowland's sights. One early morning when Zeff went out the front door of his waterfront home in Westport, the state police were waiting for him with a search warrant. Zeff ran to the back of the house and out the back door—even though you might think that an attorney would know that the state police wouldn't show up at the front door without having the back and side doors covered too. Zeff ran past the police carrying two Gap shopping bags. He ran to the hedge bordering his neighbor's property, and although the police shouted for him to stop he threw a bag over the hedge.

At that point the police again yelled for him to stop, but he didn't. Zeff threw the second bag over the hedge as well, apparently believing that because the police didn't have a warrant for his neighbor's property he could somehow get away with getting rid of some incriminating evidence. Great plan! (The police later retrieved the bags from the neighbor.)

It turned out that the two bags were filled with audiotapes. Zeff had been recording every telephone conversation he had had during the past three years. After the police evaluated the tapes, I received a telephone call requesting that I come to the state police barracks and meet with them.

I called Thomas Puccio, a well-known criminal attorney who had been doing some work for Mirage Resorts. He had an extraordinary record as a prosecutor and criminal defense lawyer, representing the likes of the fugitive rapist Alex Kelly, acquitted socialite murder suspect Klaus Von Bulow, and others. Puccio told me that I should call the state police back and tell them I'd be happy to meet with them, but at his office, not at the state police barracks, because the state police are famous for tipping off the press, and it wouldn't be good for a Mirage executive to be seen on the evening news walking into the police department with Thomas Puccio in tow.

The police agreed to meet me at Puccio's New York office, and when they showed up they said, "Mr. Bronson, we feel like we know you. We've heard your voice on hours and hours of phone conversations with Bob Zeff."

They were quick to point out that I wasn't a target or a subject of any investigation; they just wanted my help. The matters they were involved in didn't concern me, and during the countless hours of phone conversations I'd had with Bob Zeff over three years, I never said anything that was in any way incriminating. Ultimately, Zeff was cleared of any wrongdoing, but the state Ethics Commission fined him fifteen thousand dollars for the Muska incident and for faulty record keeping concerning his lobbying activities. His dog track went bankrupt shortly afterward. The last I checked, Frank Muska was back teaching at Western Connecticut State University, none the worse for wear.

And Mirage? Well, the Connecticut crusade turned out to be a practice run for a much more important battle: The War at the Shore.

CHAPTER 4

Gorilla Wrestling

IN LATE 1995, I was sitting limply on the sofa in my library in Greenfield Hill, just outside of Westport, Connecticut, feeling discouraged about the whole Hartford/Bridgeport casino debacle and trying to figure out what to do with the last half—make that the last third—of my life. Should I go back to developing shopping centers and office buildings? Take another chance in gaming? Work on my golf game and try to get my handicap down to a new low? Or maybe—

The phone rang. Edie picked it up in the kitchen. "Skip, it's Steve."

"Hey, Skip!" Steve said, radiating charm and good cheer. "How are you doing? *What* are you doing?"

"Well, Steve, to tell you the truth I'm sitting here thinking about the Connecticut project."

"Yeah? So am I."

I started to apologize. I'd spent $10 million of our company's money and four agonizing years and couldn't close the deal. Steve cut me off.

"Screw those people in Connecticut!" he said. "Forget about it! We've got a better opportunity in Atlantic City."

I thought to myself: "Is he serious?" If this had been a bad sitcom I'd have held the receiver at arm's length and stared at it in disbelief; but I just listened, too surprised to reply.

"This is great. I'm *happy* about this," Steve said. And I realized with even greater shock that he wasn't just trying to put a positive spin on things, he actually *was* happy.

"This is great!" he said. "We gave it a shot; it didn't work. But now this is perfect, because you know something? This is better for us, and you'll head this thing up."

That finally unlocked my jaw. "But Steve—"

"We've got this terrific opportunity in Atlantic City," he said, in case I'd missed his point the first time around, "and it really needs your skill set to make this thing work."

During my long career developing shopping centers, I've had the ability to create an idea, a strategy to support it, and the wherewithal to execute that strategy. I've also been able to get the critically important government entitlements that are needed to allow a project to go forward, which just may be the most crucial part of getting a project done.

Steve continued, "This is an incredible prospect for the company. The thing that's missing in this equation is *you*. *You've* gotta take your team and just shift over to Atlantic City." He gathered his breath for one last comment.

"I'm telling you this is great!" he said.

Finally, he stopped. A strange combination of relief, disbelief, exhaustion and exhilaration passed through me. It was too much to handle at that moment.

I said, "Steve, to be honest with you, I don't even know what I'm gonna do now. I'm devastated by what happened, and I need to get away. I've got to go somewhere."

"You've got to go away for a week or two? Go away," he said. "But the minute you come back, we've gotta start."

And then we talked for the next hour. I didn't realize it then, but by the time we finished, we'd filled in all the empty spaces in my calendar for the next five years of my life.

———

Steve's ability to shake off a defeat like the one we had suffered in Connecticut was remarkable, but to be honest, I hadn't been completely blindsided by his interest in Atlantic City. About six months earlier, a New Jersey lawyer, let's call him Jack Innis, had convinced Steve and me to meet with then-governor Christine Todd Whitman to discuss building something new in Atlantic City. Mirage had applied for a gaming license, which we received in June. At the time, all of my attention was focused, as it needed to be, on Connecticut. For four years I had been consumed with what I was doing in my native state, a 12-rounder that ended in frustration. But unlike boxing, where you have a few months to recoup from one battle and prepare for the next, we had to jump right back in the fray. At least this time around, we wouldn't have to worry about convincing people to legalize gaming.

In the book *Monopoly* author Rod Kennedy, Jr. points out that in 1935, Parker Bros. introduced a real estate trading game that has gone on to become the world's bestselling board game with more than 250 million copies sold in 80 countries. One of the unexpected side effects of Monopoly's extraordinary success was to make famous the streets of Atlantic City, New Jersey. It would be difficult to find a child or adult who is not familiar with Baltic Avenue, St. James Place or certainly the prime real estate properties of Park Place and Boardwalk.

Forty years after the Monopoly craze had begun, even the most die-hard fan wouldn't want to walk down the fabled streets at night. The city had hosted the 1964 Democratic Convention, but had been unable to turn the corner. New Jersey passed a law in 1976 allowing casino gambling as a last-ditch effort to save the crumbling resort town. Unfortunately, Atlantic City never managed to become the Las Vegas of the East Coast. There weren't enough direct flights or hotel rooms to make it a prime spot for conventions. People will come to Las Vegas not just to gamble, but also to see a show, dine out at a renowned restaurant or relax by an extravagant pool. Most people bussed into Atlantic City to play the slots for a few hours before heading home. It wasn't a destination; just a pit stop.

Steve and Atlantic City had a somewhat unsteady relationship. Shortly after New Jersey legalized casino gaming, Steve purchased an old motel on the Boardwalk, rebuilt it into a glittering jewel, and named it the Golden Nugget, the same as his then-flagship property in Las Vegas. The Golden Nugget Atlantic City was the best-run and most profitable hotel-casino in town (despite having the least amount of gaming space). Steve treated his employees well, and almost without exception they loved working there.

The problem wasn't with the operation, but with the politicians who controlled gaming in New Jersey. They'd set up a creaky and onerous bureaucracy whose regulators were ridiculous nitpickers and as slow as geology. For instance, each one of the Golden Nugget's employees, from chambermaids and busboys up to Steve himself, had to go through endless background checks and when on duty had to wear enough I.D. badges and licenses to make an Elks Club conventioneer look well-dressed. The state was so paranoid about mob influence in its casinos that, during the 1980 ribbon cutting for Steve's Golden Nugget, then-New Jersey Governor Brendan Byrne, who sounded a bit like Christopher Walken, issued a memorable warning to organized crime: "Keep

your filthy hands off Atlantic City. Keep the hell out of our state."
His timing, at the opening of one of the town's completely legiti-
mate operations, was a slap in the face. Byrne is known for his
sense of humor, but there was nothing funny about his grand-
standing and innuendo.

Steve was still smarting from that ridiculous self-serving
remark when we sat down with Governor Whitman. Actually, he
was frustrated that the millions he'd already invested in the city
had done so little to improve the lives of the largely impoverished
people who lived there. This wasn't pure altruism: to high rollers,
driving through traffic-choked streets and nasty neighborhoods
to get to their gaming tables was a turn-off. Every city has bad
areas, but in Atlantic City, the slums are practically in the hotels'
backyards. One moment you can be sipping Champagne under a
jewel-saturated chandelier, the next you step out of your hotel and
witness a drug deal going down while a parade of prostitutes lead
their johns to a dingy motel that only rents rooms by the hour.

The juxtaposition of decadence and decay is astounding. The
roaming casinos are right up against houses not nearly large
enough to accommodate all the people who are sheltered inside.
There is no rhyme or reason to the layout or the architecture. It
is a hodge-podge of styles similar to the collage of Los Angeles,
but in Atlantic City, the buildings are the worst every period has
to offer. Some houses are squeezed in next to each other, others
stand isolated on a field of overgrown yellow grass, a stripped
truck the only ornamentation in the backyard. The one consistent
theme is the dullness of the colors. All the buildings seem faded:
tired grays and morose browns, the walls smother and diffuse
the light.

Las Vegas is in the middle of the desert; Atlantic City is on the
ocean. Las Vegas is a four-hour drive from Los Angeles. Atlantic
City is two hours outside of New York and only an hour away

from Philadelphia. On paper, you'd give the nod to A.C.; in reality, it doesn't do anywhere near the same amount of business as its cousin out West. Despite the presence of casinos, Atlantic City had been unable to prosper, in large part because most of the gaming revenue promised for Atlantic City's revitalization wound up diverted away from the city that generated it and into the state's general fund. Politicians in cities such as Trenton, Newark and Jersey City—the more populous northern half of New Jersey—held most of the political power. Southern New Jersey, which included Atlantic City, was treated as a poor, powerless cousin. It didn't help that New Jersey was among the most crooked states in the nation. Governors, state legislators and mayors regularly wound up in court for one kind of civic malfeasance or another. They didn't retire; they just went straight to jail. In 1987 a disgusted Steve Wynn decided to take a big profit by accepting a $440 million offer from Hilton for the Golden Nugget and bid Atlantic City good riddance.

In the meantime, Donald Trump, the boisterous New York developer, had become a force in the city. He had taken his father's real estate business and built it into a company even those who knew little about the business knew about. Donald was a big guy, with big hair, a big voice, and most notably, a big personality. He was more than a tycoon; he was an instant headline. A year after making a huge splash in Manhattan with the famous Trump Tower, he set his sights on Atlantic City, opening the Trump Plaza in 1984, followed by Trump Castle (subsequently named Trump Marina) and the Taj Mahal in 1990. Though he controlled a quarter of the town's casinos, the gaming establishments were hardly Trump's most valuable assets. Like most of the other joints in town, they were struggling.

Innis had a history with Steve in Atlantic City, and wanted to bring Steve and his money back to New Jersey, even though Steve had dismissed Atlantic City as "just a big, overregulated gambling joint" where the state government stifled, rather than encouraged, new development. But nearly twenty years after gaming had been introduced, the state realized that in order to compete with the new Indian casinos that began cropping up, the city needed to transform itself into an attractive destination, bring in some new energy and create more than just big-box buildings with slot machines inside.

There were no casinos in Atlantic City that compared to the Las Vegas hotels like the Mirage or the MGM Grand. The New Jersey resorts more closely resembled the kind of establishments that sit on the edge of the Nevada-California border, run-down, no-frills places capitalizing on convenience not amenities. Location, not execution. They were glorified motels several generations behind the industry standard and unlikely to make up the difference.

———

Steve's then-wife Elaine has a knack for summing things up quite succinctly. During the push for a casino in Bridgeport, she came out to meet a local power broker who was not in favor of gaming, and he proceeded to tell us all the reasons he knew that a casino was exactly the wrong idea for a murder capital with the historic old nickname of—I kid you not—"The Park City." Elaine responded by eloquently dispelling, point by point, all the myths, half-truths and outright misinformation he espoused. When we got back into the car she looked at me and smiled.

"How long until we're in New York City?" she said.

"Only fifty-five minutes," I told her

"Can you make it in fifty?" she asked, laughing.

When Elaine came to visit Atlantic City, we took a walk down the Boardwalk with Charlie Meyerson, a casino host who went back with Steve to the days of the Atlantic City Golden Nugget. Everybody in the casino business knew Charlie. He was a legend. The Boardwalk, despite its pseudo-glamorous name, is not a place where anyone is having fun. It is a dilapidated stretch of cracked and creaking wood held together by a mosaic of cigarette butts. It runs across several casinos, though at night it's desolate, with only a few characters immune to its sadness drifting about and peddling their wares. Elaine looked around and said, "It's the same people, they're just older"; the point being that since Steve left town, the casinos hadn't been able to generate many new customers; the city was stuck in the past.

A lot of people in Atlantic City, including casino operators such as Donald Trump, who'd arrived later, labeled Steve a deserter, a traitor, and worse. But Jack Innis assured Steve that this was ancient history. Steve, he said, was remembered fondly by all the local politicians—those who hadn't been indicted—and by his former casino workers. Plus, a well-publicized overhaul of the regulatory board a few years earlier was the real deal. As far as the New Jersey political cesspool was concerned, he and Christie Whitman, who had too much personal integrity and too big a family fortune to accept bribes, had all that under control.

Real estate development takes a great deal of time. If you pass a pharmacy on the street, it's not as if someone decided that would be a good location for a drugstore, snapped his fingers and built one just like that. There is a lot of lead time that goes into every effort. Finding an architect is relatively simple, as is finding a site and securing the finances if you have good credit, but all that is merely a precursor to the toughest part of the job: getting the right to build. There's a ton of different approvals that are necessary from curb cuts to environmental tests. There are a lot of different agencies to juggle and bureaucrats to convince, and while you're waiting on one approval you have to make sure you haven't lost another. Some look at a building and wonder about how long it took to build, I look at the same project and think about how long it took to get the right to build. And that's just for something as simple as a corner drugstore.

Developing a casino is exhilarating, but not in the instant gratification sense of the word. Take the red tape involved in building a pharmacy and multiply it by 1,000. It's a grueling process filled with numerous ups and downs. Only one detail has to go wrong somewhere along the line and a long-planned endeavor can go out the window in a heartbeat. In a perfect world, where there are no lawsuits to battle and the government rolls out the proverbial red carpet for you, putting together a 2,000-plus-room hotel-casino takes 3½ years. There's a year to design it and 30 months to build it. That's in a perfect world without any litigation or politicking hiccups. Jack Innis assured us that we were stepping into such an ideal situation. Nothing could be further from the truth.

———

Speaking of architects and design, Steve had recently been invited by Frank Gehry to Bilbao, Spain to see Gehry's masterpiece, The Guggenheim Museum of Bilbao. After seeing Gehry's handiwork, Steve mentioned to me that no iconic architect (or "starchitect" as they are now known) had ever designed a casino hotel. When Steve mentioned to Gehry that we were going to do a project in Atlantic City and asked if he might be interested in designing it, Gehry said he would but what he really would like to do was to collaborate with the renowned architect Phillip Johnson. Steve, of course, said that would be incredible as Johnson was probably the most famous living architect at the time.

Steve retained their services and a month later he and I flew to the offices of Johnson-Burgee to meet with Gehry and Johnson.

They had created a model of the proposed Atlantic City project. When they took us into the conference room to see it, Steve had difficulty hiding his displeasure. He didn't like what appeared to be a large tin can that had been run through a blender. He particularly disliked the fact that it was sited at the front edge of the property. He went into a long diatribe where he explained that good architecture is all about contradiction, that the reason the Mirage was so successful was because it was a tropical themed resort in the middle of a desert, the last thing you would expect to see. He said, "You need to understand that good architecture is all about tension. And you've missed the point." He also correctly noted that the swimming pool would be out of the sun in the afternoon.

Steve was never known to be a shrinking violet, and his monologue took on a really negative tone. I could tell by looking at the faces of Phillip Johnson and Frank Gehry that they were none too pleased. At that point Steve asked to use the restroom and one of Mr. Johnson's assistants led Steve to it. I was then left in the room with the two world-renowned architects. Frank Gehry said, "The last thing I need is an architecture lesson from a casino guy. We're out of here." He proceeded to pack up his papers and stormed out of the room. Phillip Johnson began to follow.

I grabbed Johnson by the arm and said, "Mr. Johnson, please don't confuse his enthusiasm with arrogance. Design is critically important to Steve and he's extremely passionate about the look of his hotels. Please wait until he gets back so that we can discuss this further." With that, Phillip Johnson looked at me and said, "Young man, I've made it 90 years without this guy . . . I can make it the rest of the way."

At that point Steve returned from the men's room. When he realized that Johnson and Gehry were not there he asked me what happened. I told him exactly what they had to say. Steve looked at me and said, "Well that's good because I hated what they came up with. And by the way, they'd better not send us a bill for that piece of shit."

———

My experience working in Atlantic City had been primarily as a fight promoter, not a developer. In the late 1970s, a number of developers were buying sports teams. Among others, Mel and Herb Simon had just bought the NBA's Indiana Pacers, and another well-known shopping center developer, Youngstown, Ohio's Edward J. DeBartolo, bought the Pittsburgh Penguins National Hockey League franchise and the San Francisco 49ers of the National Football League. Owning a sports franchise was a good way to raise your profile, and since networking is a key aspect of development, getting involved in sports seemed like a good business move.

Along with Shelley Finkel, a property management company I had formed, Monitor Management, teamed up with Main Events (the Duva family's firm) and put together a boxing promotion called "A Night of Gold." It featured the champions from the USA's stellar 1984 team: Mark Breland, Meldrick Taylor, Pernell Whitaker and Tyrell Biggs (in order to close the deal, Breland, the main attraction, insisted we take on his shy, bronze-winning roommate, one Evander Holyfield). Breland was a tall, good-looking welterweight with superb skills and a punch to match. If there were such a thing as a can't miss prospect, he was it. Or so we thought. His promising career was derailed by a loss to the unknown Hartford native Marlon "Moochie" Starling. The star of our class turned out to be Evander "Real Deal" Holyfield, who beefed himself up from a cruiserweight and became one of the best heavyweights of his generation. The Main Events/Monitor 1991 Atlantic City fight between Holyfield and

George Foreman, "The Battle of the Ages," set a then pay-per-view record of over $80 million. The fight between Holyfield and Foreman was nothing comparing to the showdown Steve Wynn and Donald Trump were about to be involved in.

———

I sometimes wonder what would have happened if I'd turned Steve down. Then I think of a quote from Robert Strauss, the former chairman of the Democratic National Committee, who described what it's like to wrestle a gorilla. He said, "You don't quit when you're tired. You quit when the gorilla's tired."

Gorilla wrestling or otherwise, I'm not the quitting type. So exactly one week after my self-prescribed time off, I got into my car and drove 5½ hours from my Connecticut home toward Atlantic City. I was accompanied by Victor Cruse and Bruce Goldman, my right arm and my left arm on the Connecticut project.

Like me, they were New England natives and accustomed to the politics and practices of Connecticut. We would be spending several years—most of that time away from our families—surrounded by strangers. Halfway to Atlantic City, we stopped to get gas on the New Jersey Turnpike at a rest area known as the Cheesequake Service Center. As we ate lunch there at a dirty Burger King, I had a premonition that we were heading into something we'd regret.

New Jersey is nicknamed the Garden State, but you wouldn't guess that driving down the turnpike. Factories and oil refineries fill the landscape and the sky vacillates between overcast gray and hazy shades of polluted pink. If you were looking for a place to film a post-apocalyptic world, it wouldn't be a bad place to start.

In Atlantic City, we traveled the last few miles along surface streets lined with hookers and the homeless. My mind flashed to

Bridgeport and the urban decay I had seen there. But this was worse. Bridgeport didn't have a casino to pump money into the economy. Atlantic City had venues such as Park Place and the Taj Mahal, but the town was in shambles nonetheless. Bridgeport was an example of what could've been. Atlantic City looked like what couldn't be.

Victor and I moved into a company-owned house on 111 S. Cornwall in the Ventnor neighborhood that Steve had lived in when he spent two weeks of each month working at the Atlantic City Golden Nugget. It was never sold, and because it was just an afterthought, the company hadn't spent any money to keep it up after Steve left. Although it was on the ocean, it was musty and rundown and the way it was sited meant you couldn't actually see the ocean from any window. This didn't change the fact that you could smell the rotten clams washed up on the shore no matter what room you were in. At the time, I remember thinking that it was just about the bleakest day of my life.

I was wrong.

In Las Vegas, the different companies don't usually interfere with each other's projects. The higher the overall quality of the hotels and casinos, the more desirable the city becomes and the better off the industry is as a whole. I thought that the environment would be similar in Atlantic City; but my first week in town, Lou Toscano from the mayor's office took me aside and warned me that our competitors were laying in wait. They were jealous of Steve and ready to make things as difficult as they could for Mirage. We wouldn't be squaring off against prudish politicians or insurance companies, but rather our fellow gaming companies. It was going to be a civil war. Any optimism stemming from the thought that there would be fewer obstacles than we had encountered in Connecticut dissipated instantly. So much for the hero's welcome.

CHAPTER 5

Anyone for Tunnel?

IT'S IMPOSSIBLE to pin down exactly when the big Steve Wynn-Donald Trump feud began. Some trace it to a golf game between the two at Shadow Creek. Others think it began in the early 1990s, when Steve convinced a key Trump employee, casino executive Dennis Gomes, to come to work for Mirage in Las Vegas. Donald sued Steve for millions over that one, claiming that Steve induced Gomes to break his employment contract. They settled out of court.

Though both Steve and Donald are wildly successful, their principle talents are quite different. While Steve has appeared in several commercials (most notably a few with Frank Sinatra back in the days of the Golden Nugget Atlantic City), he would never talk about himself the way Donald discusses "Trump." Of course, such self-promotion goes well beyond ego-stroking. It's actually an ingenious business tool. Trump has succeeded in making a brand out of his name, and whether people have positive or negative impressions of him, there's no arguing the power of his personality and the impact he's had on celebrity culture. Steve's

professional acumen is measured in the consistently strong per-
formance of his endeavors, while the volatility of Trump's fortunes
is equally well-known, and in an odd way, may even add to his legend. Donald has pursued a variety of different projects—he seems
to always be on the lookout for a new type of venture—but Steve
has basically stuck to hotel-casinos. Each man is so fervent in his
own way that the slightest detail could've sparked a first-class
media war.

All I can tell you is that I was at the opening of the Mirage
Hotel in Vegas in 1989 and was with Steve and Elaine when they
gave Donald and his then-wife Ivana a personal tour of the place,
put them up in one of the best suites, and in general acted like they
were best buddies. Of course, that was when Steve was operating
exclusively in Nevada and Donald had the East Coast gaming market to himself.

By the time Steve returned to Atlantic City in 1995, they hated
each other with a passion. Make no mistake about it: Donald
thought Steve was peeing on his spot. The former king of Atlantic
City was aiming to reclaim his title, and the current titleholder was
none too pleased about it. Trump kept saying derogatory things
about Steve in public, and that made him mad and even more determined to push his project to completion. A man like Steve does-
n't need any extra motivation to begin with; but Trump had given
him an added incentive.

Throughout the decade there was plenty of name-calling on
both sides. It was the type of language you might expect to hear
in a bar fight, but it came from two of the country's most successful businessmen. In a *New Yorker* article by Chris Smith, Donald
speculated about Steve's mental health, and Steve responded in
kind, asking: "What is the matter with him? How deeply is he dis-
turbed? When he was a kid growing up—who did this to him? I
mean, a psychiatrist would know all this."[1]

Steve and Donald weren't the only ones getting into it. If you were living in Atlantic City, you were on one side or other. Cats or dogs, Beatles or Stones, Trump or Wynn? Our ally Lou Toscano said, "Donald is a soap opera; Steve Wynn is a Shakespeare play." [2] Those in the Trump camp had their own metaphors, and Donald kept churning out the insults and allegations.

But it was really all about business. And deep down, Donald Trump is quite simply a very savvy businessman. I've come to know him pretty well the past few years, and beneath the bluster and the big hair, he knows how to buy and sell real estate, how to build a building, including the finite cost of a piece of steel and a ton of concrete. And he certainly knew how to read his balance sheet in Atlantic City.

His biggest problem—one that was seldom, if ever, mentioned at the time—was his price of money. Few people realize that one of the biggest expenses in any real estate development project is the cost of borrowing cash. Lots and lots of it. Amazing but true: a project's interest costs can be larger than the cost of land, and sometimes even close to the cost of construction. So if I want to build a hotel-casino project and I can borrow money at 5 percent, but your credit isn't as good and you have to pay 10 percent, it's going to cost you about twice as much as me to build the same number of hotel rooms. Or to put it a different way, I can build a stellar hotel-casino for the same cost that you can build a mediocre hotel-casino, because my money only costs half as much as your money. If you have great investment-grade credit, like Mirage did, you've got a tremendous advantage.

In this case it meant that Donald, running his Trump Plaza, Trump Castle and Trump Taj Mahal hotels, had no hope of matching Mirage's cost of either building or upgrading in Atlantic City. So the smart move, as he knew perfectly well, was to prevent Mirage from getting started at all. In this fight he had two things going for him: he could throw up as many roadblocks as he wanted, and only one of them had to hold.

———

In 1987—the year Steve Wynn left Atlantic City—the local government tried to auction off a 178-acre piece of land known as the H-Tract. The exact number of bids was zero. Zilch. Nada. Eight years later, there still weren't any takers and the government was ready to give it away. The site was a dump. Literally. It had been a landfill and would require significant cleanup before it was usable. But where others saw a wasteland, Steve saw the perfect location for a glittering mega-resort in the mold of the Bellagio, his latest and most expensive Las Vegas project that was then in the early stages of development.

Mirage had been scouting the H-Tract, but we were not the only company to have an interest in the land. Donald Trump had his own plans for the heretofore-neglected real estate. Eight years of silence, and then seemingly out of nowhere two of the heaviest hitters in gaming take a liking to the same site.

The H-Tract is located in the marina district, a few miles northeast of the Boardwalk, which for generations had been the beating heart of Atlantic City and where most of the existing casinos were located. If Mirage developed the first real Las Vegas-style hotel-casino in the marina, and if we were subsequently joined by other gaming companies, it could shift the pulse of Atlantic City away from the Boardwalk, much the same way the Mirage had moved the focus of Las Vegas from Downtown to the Strip.

The H-Tract was large enough to accommodate several projects, and Steve, being a more-the-merrier kind of guy, looked for partners. In July, Mirage and Circus Circus (which owned properties such as Excalibur and Luxor in Las Vegas) submitted a proposal for a complex that was far more ambitious than anything else in Atlantic City. There were already a dozen casinos in town, but none of them came close to offering what Steve had planned: two hotels, 4,000 rooms and a cost of upwards of $1 billion. The city only received one other proposal for the H-Tract. Donald Trump and Harrah's wanted to create a $25 million golf course.

Neither Mirage nor Trump offered any money for the land. However, both sides promised to transform largely empty space into something that would advance the local economy. The numbers were overwhelmingly on our side. The casino would create thousands of jobs, the golf course, but a fraction of that. The casino would generate over $100 million in taxes annually, whereas the golf course wouldn't pay anywhere near that amount. What's more, Trump's proposal relied heavily on funds from the Casino Reinvestment Development Authority (CRDA), an organization that used gaming revenue to improve the city. It was like choosing between a town fair and Disneyland.

When it was put to a vote, the City Council decided to go with the casino. It was a shutout: 9-0. City Councilman Lorenzo T. Langford said, "For me, this was, as they say, a no-brainer."[3] Round One went to Mirage, but it was the last easy win we'd have.

———

There wasn't any time to savor the victory. We had a very serious problem. All roads lead to Rome, but nothing led to the marina. The area was cut off from the rest of town. The Atlantic City Expressway, which was the main route into the city, dead-ended at the Boardwalk. In order to get to the H-Tract, a driver would have to snake his way through a maze of surface streets, navigating one of the worst neighborhoods in the country. There was no way a casino, no matter how spectacular, could flourish under such circumstances. Quite simply, the infrastructure was not there.

Steve came to Atlantic City a few weeks after winning the right to develop the H-Tract. It's one thing to see a piece of property when your interest in it is purely speculative, it's another when you have it and you're getting around to the business of building something tangible. The rosy tint fades away and every flaw is magnified. As Steve and I drove through the seedy labyrinth, the isolation of the H-Tract set in.

"This is awful," he said. "We can't build on this land; it's not going to work. This is a disaster!" Though we hadn't made much headway with the project, Steve had gotten excited about his return to Atlantic City. Now it looked like that return would be over before it began.

Steve is prone to such outbursts, but he wouldn't have gotten where he is if he were one to give up easily. After the initial frustration subsided, he gathered the engineers and set about finding an answer to our problem. Steve considered a number of solutions and devised a plan based on the least drastic option: With its cut of the projected gaming revenue, the state could help finance a new exit from the expressway and a new road, most of it hidden underground in a tunnel that would go to our site.

Steve believed in spending as much money as necessary to build hotel-casinos that measured up to his incredibly high standards. However, he believed just as strongly that public roads—and in this case a tunnel—were the responsibility of local, state or federal governments. His mantra: "Government must spend its money to provide the necessary infrastructure so that private enterprise will risk its capital." He told me that Jack Innis had assured him this would be no problem. And that's why Steve had dispatched his brother Kenny, who ran the company's construction division, to get things started on both the political and construction fronts.

However, when I got to Atlantic City, I discovered that Innis's guarantee had about as much weight as a golf ball on the moon. I don't know whom he had talked to about the tunnel, or even *if* he had talked to anyone about it, but it was far from a settled issue. It was "no problem" only if you considered a powder keg to be a mere nuisance. After some phone calls and quiet meetings with local politicians to assess the lay of the land, I'd learned that although Kenny Wynn and his crew had made some progress in the engineering department, they'd completely neglected the most critical component of the whole plan: garnering the support of the people in charge of voting to authorize the construction of Steve's proposed tunnel. This was like buying a set of tires when you don't own a car. If the community is not in your corner, it doesn't matter how great your plans are, they'll never see the light of day. It didn't take me long to find out that there was going to be serious opposition from the local residents, an overwhelming resistance that Innis had failed to either gauge or disclose.

———

Innis was around 60, a lanky cigar smoker and smart. He and I—like Sidney Poitier and Tony Curtis in the movie *The Defiant Ones*—were shackled together for the foreseeable future. He would never look you in the eye. This might have been good judgment on his part. You know the expression, "You look in his eyes and there's nobody home?" That wasn't Jack's problem. There was a whole lot going on inside there, probably more than most people could handle.

For some reason, Innis appeared to be afraid of Steve Wynn. Absolutely terrified. However, Steve rarely came to Atlantic City as he was usually preoccupied in Las Vegas; I was in charge of spearheading the casino. Innis seemed thrilled when Steve effectively made me the CEO of the project, because then he could deal only with me instead of having to deal with Steve.

Innis's specialty, his *modus operandi* if you will, was to constantly assure me that everything was going perfectly well, meanwhile he kept the legal bills coming in hot and heavy. And his bills had a lot of commas.

I'd ask him, "Jack, is that councilman (or state senator or assemblyman) on our side?" and he would invariably answer "You bet!" or "No problem!" or, "I've got it under control." If I countered with, "But Jack—I just saw that councilman on the evening news, and he said Mirage's development of the H-Tract would be 'catastrophic,'" Jack would shift his eyes away, put his arm around my shoulder and condescendingly tell me: "That's just the line he has to give his constituents. I've talked to him privately, and he promised that when the time comes and the chips are down he'll . . ." Blah, blah, blah.

In fact, if Innis and I ever got a reluctant lawmaker in a corner, Jack would flatter the guy so much that he'd be too embarrassed or disgusted to tell me what he really thought. I considered firing Innis many times, but in the end I figured he had just enough history and power in Atlantic City that it was worth it to keep him on. While he didn't have enough clout to put the project across the goal line, without him I thought the whole thing might come crashing down on our heads.

With Innis, the gates were down, the lights were flashing, but there was no train coming. My solution was to bypass him and, whenever possible, talk directly to the principal players. This not only increased my workload tremendously, but was nearly impossible, since he would frequently show up unannounced when I'd "forget" to notify him of a meeting with some important politician or bureaucrat. That meant little would be accomplished.

One of the few helpful things Innis did was to introduce me

to some of the local politicians. Our chief ally in Atlantic City was Mayor James Whelan. I have no qualms in stating that I loved James Whelan. He was a walking, talking oxymoron: an honest Atlantic City mayor. Many of his predecessors were either in jail or under indictment, but he wouldn't even let you buy him lunch or a movie ticket. Whelan, about six-foot-six, was a Democrat who'd been a lifeguard, a swimming instructor and a schoolteacher before entering politics. He wore close-cropped hair, a finely trimmed beard and round glasses. He walked with the slight hunch common among tall people accustomed to bending down to hear conversations and fit in photographs.

The mayor, with the help of his chief of staff Lou Toscano, was a great strategist and political tactician, but it was all in the service of doing what was best for his beaten-down city. This included getting Mirage's hotel built and improving the local economy. He got tremendous heat from many of his constituents for siding with us, but he handled it all with patience and aplomb.

If anything, he was more worried for me than for himself. After months of watching me be abused by our opponents, he peered down at me from way up there and, concerned for my health and sanity, said, "Are you *sure* you want to go through with this?" When I said I was, he told me he would be with me all the way—then confidently bet me five dollars that the tunnel to the H-Tract—dubbed the "Brigantine Connector" because the Atlantic City dump was adjacent to the nearby town of Brigantine, which didn't have direct access to the expressway—would never be built.

There was one introduction Innis wouldn't make for me. I had to meet our chief legislative ally, State Senator William Gormley, on my own. I liked Bill Gormley for a lot of reasons. The most important one was because he was a shrewd politician, but also because he had had a run-in with Jack Innis and they weren't on speaking terms. Apparently they had butted heads before I arrived on the scene. It was heavy lifting just getting the two of them into the same room together.

A Republican whose district included Atlantic City, Gormley was an intense and engaging man. He worked the phones with more drive than a telemarketer, constantly calling, sometimes in the middle of the night. You might get exhausted from the bombardment, but if the calls slowed down, all of a sudden you'd worry that you were out of the loop and you'd actually miss the deluge. He was a former marine and a natural politician, and if you peered closely into his eyes you could see the wheels going around back there. Solidly built, he looked like the last guy you'd want to take a punch from, though he was anything but crude; an impeccable dresser, he never had a hair out of place and bore a passing resemblance to Disney's Robert Iger. The word about Bill Gormley was that he was one of the smartest politicians in South Jersey— although that was a lot like saying he was a doctor with good penmanship.

Gormley, who chaired the powerful Judiciary Committee, told me he was a staunch supporter of Steve Wynn; wanted him back in Atlantic City badly; and understood perfectly that construction and operation of a new Mirage resort would mean thousands of jobs for his constituents. He was essential in introducing and pushing the bills we needed passed by the New Jersey legislature. And most importantly—this was certainly not the rule in New Jersey politics—he worked with us for free. We weren't going to bribe the lawmakers for their votes.

In Whitman, Whelan and Gormley, I had strong political support to complement my team. I wanted to keep things on the down low, so I ran a small operation. When you're trying to push a controversial idea through a community reluctant to change, you need to make sure your message is being heard, but there's a delicate balance between having a presence and having too big a presence. The last thing I needed was for the local residents to feel that Mirage was invading their city. We were outsiders, the "Vegas people" (never mind that my closest associates and I were from Connecticut), and the smaller our group, the better our chances of success.

Bill Smith was our go-between with the Mirage engineers in Las Vegas. He wore a mustache and glasses, and he was as studious as he looked. A Philly guy (which practically made him an Atlantic City guy), he had the ability to put the technical aspects of our project into layman's term and was the perfect complement to Bruce Goldman, our expert on construction and engineering matters from Connecticut. The two of them saw to the details of the Brigantine Connector, and it was up to the rest of us to actually get the thing green-lighted. Lori Campor was our all-purpose office manager. A pretty, blonde Jersey girl, she knew the ground conditions and vernacular. Secretary, scheduler, organizer; if I needed something, Lori got it done and she got it done quickly. Tony Sartor, the head of a local engineering firm PS&S, was incredibly well-connected and the best under-the-radar strategist one could ever hope to meet.

However, the most important cog in the machine was my point man, Victor Cruse. Cruse was a good-looking, solidly built and intelligent African American lawyer. He could easily be mistaken for Raiders' Hall of Fame running back Marcus Allen. Victor was very charismatic and matched his forceful personality with a great set of pipes. Had he been interested in a less controversial line of work, he could have had a career doing voice overs. He was a prosperous and popular guy in Hartford until he got caught up in a big scandal with the Department of Housing and Urban Development that unfolded that year—the whole mess ultimately was laid on the shoulders of hapless HUD secretary, Samuel Pierce, Jr.

At the time Steve and I were trying to get a casino going in Connecticut, Victor was working for a company that was developing publicly subsidized Section Eight housing. He was his company's man in Washington and it was his job to get the federal funding for its projects. That's what he did, and that's how he played some part, witting or unwitting, in some of the funny stuff that was happening. Victor was indicted then found not guilty, but he had to spend all the money he had defending himself.

One day I was at the Hartford Civic Center to watch a University of Connecticut basketball game. As I was walking to my seat I saw Victor Cruse; he'd been in the news every day and I recognized him immediately.

I walked up to him and said, "Hey, how are you doing?"

He said, "I'm not doing so well."

"You went through a hard time."

He shook his head and smiled. "Oh man, you don't *know* what I've been through. You don't have a clue what I've been through."

But he knew who I was, and we talked a little bit about Billy DiBella, and as we talked I saw a certain sparkle in his eye and I thought: "What a cool guy."

When I got home that night I phoned Billy and said, "Hey, I met Victor Cruse."

He said, "Skip, the guy's very talented. I think he got screwed on this HUD deal."

I said, "What if I hire him and make him a lobbyist and have him work for me and let him do all the outreach in the black community so that I can get my casino project done?"

"You couldn't have a better guy to do that," Billy said. "He'd be perfect."

Victor did a good job in Connecticut, but his skills were even more valuable in Atlantic City. He was a chameleon. If we were in a meeting with some high-ranking politicos, he could be as diplomatic as a UN delegate; but if he was down on the street, he could communicate equally well with the down-on-their luck Atlantic City residents. Not only was he essential in leading our grass roots campaign, but he was also a good friend. My "brother from another mother," Victor was an avid golfer and a Hartford native. When one of us got down, the other was there to help him up.

All in all, it was a talented, determined team, and it needed to be in order to withstand the kind of pressure we were about to face.

———

Eminent domain gives the government the authority to purchase private property that would otherwise not be up for sale (anything from a house to a factory) when, and only when, such a transaction benefits the public. It is a controversial but necessary part of just about every major real estate project. Were it not for eminent domain, there would be no interstate highway system. You just can't build something of a certain magnitude without inconveniencing a few people. No one wants to be forced to sell their homes, but it's often an inevitable step in the evolution of a community.

Horace Bryant Jr. Drive, named after a deceased city commissioner and pioneering African American Atlantic City politician, was in the middle of a tiny neighborhood on the city's west side. This was one of the few middle-class African American neighborhoods in Atlantic City; it was populated by maybe a hundred or so relatively affluent black homeowners. For maximum impact, its defenders called it "Striver's Row," after the famous street in Harlem where so many black doctors, lawyers and entertainers such as Eubie Blake and W.C. Handy lived. Nobody that was particularly rich or famous lived on Horace Bryant Jr. Drive. However, it had another claim to fame. The Brigantine Connector would be built directly underneath it.

In order to build our tunnel we'd need to raze or relocate nine—count 'em, nine—private homes on Horace Bryant. When the tunnel got state and city approval, the government, paying market value, would have the right to seize the houses via eminent domain. But nobody wanted things to get that far. Before Jefferson's famed inalienable rights, there was the Locke-Smith ideal "Life, liberty and the pursuit of property." Owning land always was and always will be at the core of our society. A person's property is not something I ever take lightly, and I knew the nine homes were a major obstacle. What I hadn't anticipated was how deep the animosity would go.

Even with the governor in favor of our plan, the whole idea hinged on the outcome of a vote by the predominantly black Atlantic City Council, which seemed predisposed to stopping a project that would displace the residents of a small black neighborhood. No one in the Mirage camp seemed to grasp that basic reality.

I canvassed the nine council members (unfortunately the mayor didn't have a vote), made my best pitch and counted the votes again and again. Whichever way I added them up, we lost 5-4 every time. And that was a deal buster. The math was simple. No tunnel, no Steve, no casino.

CHAPTER 6

That Domain Thing

ONE OF THE MOST important parts of becoming a successful developer is learning the rules of the business. Rule One: There are no rules. Rule Two: In case of disputes or difficulties, see Rule One.

Let me put it another way. Years ago, when I developed the regional headquarters building in Bloomfield, Connecticut, for McDonald's Corporation, I met their regional vice president—his name was Frank Behan—and one day he showed me the manual they have for running a McDonald's restaurant. I'm paraphrasing, but in essence it read: "Six a.m. put key in door. 6:01 a.m., turn on fryer. 6:02 a.m., activate oven." Their philosophy is that if you can read you can run a McDonald's—you just have to follow their manual.

But there was no manual for the kind of work I was doing in Atlantic City. There never is. That's the basis of my love-hate relationship with the whole development business. It's exciting and terrifying, sometimes both at the same time. You get clocked a lot, but you also get to shake off the jabs and body blows and hit the other guy back. Some things work, some things don't work. But just because you've never tried something before—or even if it didn't work the first time—there's no reason not to give it a shot.

Throughout my career I've had to try a variety of maneuvers. When I was starting out as a developer in Connecticut, one of the main tools in my skill set was pure youthful audacity. Kmart has really taken a beating lately, but back in the 1970s, it was the fastest growing chain in the country. However, it wasn't yet in New England and I wanted to develop stores for them in Connecticut. Kmart had six regional real estate reps across the country, and they all had one thing in common: they never took phone calls from developers they hadn't already met or done business with.

I am an avid newspaper reader and I would constantly cut out articles about the business climate in Connecticut or the success of other chains here and mail them to the Kmart real estate guys. I tried to get through on the phone to them for months, calling at least once a week. All I needed, I figured, was to pique their interest enough for a single reply.

One day my secretary said Bob Combs was on the phone. Combs was one of Kmart's real estate reps, based in Atlanta. I wrestled my excitement and panic to a standstill and said, as calmly as I could, "Put him through."

He said: "Mr. Bronson, you've got to be the most determined guy in the world. Let me ask you a question."

"Sure," I said. At this point I was waiting for him to ask me about my shopping center experience.

"Have you ever seen Gordie Howe play hockey?"

"Sure," I said, thinking, "Huh?"

Howe, the star of the Detroit Red Wings for many years and one of the greatest hockey players ever to lace up a pair of skates, had recently been signed by my hometown Hartford Whalers (now the Carolina Hurricanes). As far as I knew, the man they called "Mr. Hockey" wasn't involved in either discount retail nor the shopping mall development business.

Combs said he'd grown up in Detroit and idolized Gordie Howe.

OK, I thought. Now I have an inkling of where this was going.

"Have you ever met him?" I asked.

"No," he said.

"Would you like to?" I asked, adding: "I can make that happen."

All the gruffness left this powerful man's voice as he asked me how I could manage it.

I said, "Well, I know the Whalers will be playing the Atlanta Flames at some point. How about I come down, we go to the game and afterward we'll have a drink with him."

Combs gulped and asked me if I was serious.

"Serious as a heart attack," I said.

He asked me meekly, "Do you think I could bring my son?"

"Absolutely," I said. "Just leave it to me."

He never said anything about real estate and neither did I. We didn't have to. There'd be plenty of time for that after I delivered the goods.

I told him I'd call him later with the details. And really, the only little detail I had to clear up was that I'd never once met Gordie Howe and he didn't know me from Adam. But I had a plan—one I'd set in motion, completely accidentally and unconsciously, about a year before.

A lot of hockey players love to play golf in their spare time and serious amateur golfers like me love to play with professional athletes. It's a rare chance to compete against pros from various sports. When owner Howard Baldwin moved the Whalers from Boston to Hartford in 1975, I sent a note to their head coach, Ron Ryan. It said: "My name is Skip Bronson. I belong to Tumble Brook Country Club. It's the best course in the area. Call me if you'd ever like to play." I got a call from Ryan a few days later, took him to play at Tumble Brook and a very nice friendship began. We've played golf together countless times through the years.

After hanging up with Combs I figured I could get Ron to do me a major favor—or at the very least, let me know the high number I would need to pay Howe to have a drink with me in Atlanta. Ryan said he would take care of the whole deal and even set me up with three great tickets to that 1977 game.

I flew to Atlanta, met Combs and his 21-year-old son, and we had a great time watching the Whalers battle the Atlanta Flames, an NHL franchise that relocated to Calgary in 1980.

After the game Gordie Howe came up to the bar in the arena, made believe he knew me and regaled us with hockey stories. (When he greeted us I was shocked at the size of his hand. It seemed as big as a catcher's mitt.) I thought the Combs boys were going to have an orgasm right there on the spot. They were in awe of this man—and frankly so was I. What a sweetheart he was, and he did it all for free.

As we were leaving the arena Bob Combs told me to come by his office in the morning. I thought it over for a nanosecond and said I was pretty sure I could make it. The next day he assigned me a territory to develop for Kmart in Middle Tennessee—which I was just about as familiar with as Outer Mongolia, but I learned quickly and the opportunity launched the next phase of my career.

———

Of course, I didn't have a sports star up my sleeve as I tried to turn the Atlantic City City Council in favor of Mirage's proposal, and to be honest, I didn't think I'd need one. I had Steve Wynn, and unlike the people in Connecticut, those in Atlantic City knew what he could do for the community. The record of the Golden Nugget Atlantic City spoke for itself, as did the bottom lines of the

A.C. casinos currently in operation. When Michael Jordan left the Bulls to play baseball for a couple of years, the team played all right, but it was a shadow of its former self. When he returned, they set the record for most wins in a season. I was basically bringing the Michael Jordan of gaming back to the Garden State. I thought I'd be welcomed with open arms; instead I was struggling to get people on board.

I was in the middle of my presentation at one community meeting when a woman stood up and said, "Mr. Bronson, we will stop you no matter what it takes, and most important, you need to know we don't want *that domain thing.*" Maybe it was because of the stress, my exhaustion, or the fact that we just needed an ice-breaker, but I started laughing. It turned out to be contagious. In a second or two the entire room was laughing. It was a brief moment of levity in an otherwise very tense confrontation.

I was prepared to make the residents some very generous offers, build a nice park over the tunnel and erect sound buffers to keep the neighborhood quiet, but the opposition remained steadfast. It had only been about a month since Rowland had sounded the death knell for the Connecticut casino and I was already finding some of my new "friends" in Atlantic City to be fickle in their support. A number of city council members said, "I'm committed to fighting this project by whatever means possible."

Pierre Hollingsworth, the president of the local NAACP chapter, rented a house on Horace Bryant. He was against the tunnel. So was a black councilman named Ernest Coursey, who said, "There is a plot to move every last one of you who looks like me out of here!" Then he added, showing that he was a reasonable guy: "We can't say to a homeowner they can't sell—but if we are pushed to the limit we will block up Horace Bryant Drive!"

Most important of all, the tunnel was adamantly opposed by Lillian Bryant, a middle-aged black woman who lived on the street and—bad news for us—was the daughter of Horace Bryant, Jr. She was always available to describe how she was fighting to keep her home and neighborhood and the hard work of her late father from being wiped out by callous white millionaires. "I will not tolerate or allow anybody to hand over my city or my home to Steve Wynn or any casino developer," she declared during one public meeting.

Presenting a compelling argument about the rejuvenation of the neighborhood was not going to be sufficient. I needed to try something new.

———

In the "Rumble in the Jungle," Muhammad Ali stayed on the ropes, picked his openings, and let the favorite, George Foreman, punch himself out. Ali scored an 8th round knockout and introduced one of the most famous tactics in boxing history.

I decided to stage my own version of Ali's "rope-a-dope" strategy. As I had learned in Connecticut, if you don't have the numbers in your favor, you don't put a measure to a vote. When it's a controversial issue—like condemning nine homes so an expensive tunnel can be built—a councilman standing on the unpopular side of the line will have a permanent target on his back. I couldn't leave my supporters hanging out to dry like that, so I decided to help them out and buy myself some time.

Our plan was to get the proposal off the table, fool our opponents into thinking that our cause was hopeless and that we'd given up. Losing 9-0 would actually be better than going down 5-4. We'd take a few months to regroup, build more support and come up with a new plan. After all, I didn't have the votes, so what did I have to lose?

I approached the mayor and asked him to officially withdraw

his support. He was befuddled, to say the least, but also somewhat relieved. Then Victor and I called the four city councilmen we had in the "yes" column and told them to change their votes.

On November 30, 1995, the City Council voted unanimously to drive a stake through the heart of Steve Wynn's audacious tunnel plan. The pendulum had swung from 4-5 against the Mirage proposal to 9-0 against us in a matter of weeks. The headline in the Atlantic City *Press* announcing our "defeat" ran the full width of the front page. In very big type it announced: "**THE TUNNEL IS DEAD.**"

———

I went to bed that night knowing the following day would start out with a rather unpleasant wakeup call. The next morning, bright and early, I got a phone call from Steve. He was furious and he asked me how such a disastrous, screwed-up thing could ever have happened to him. When I finally got a few words in, I managed to explain my plan and eventually got him to agree with my unorthodox tactics.

There were people in Steve's inner circle who were against the company's ever returning to Atlantic City. None of them wanted to leave their cozy offices at headquarters in Las Vegas and move their families 3,000 miles to a third-tier city. People don't usually like being the bearer of bad news, but there were those at Mirage who were eager to bring Steve negative reports about the New Jersey project at the first opportunity. Despite what these executives whispered in his ear, Steve was firmly committed to the project and to my judgment.

That was good to know, because we definitely had our work cut out for us. By "we" I don't mean the expensive New Jersey lobbyists I'd hired to counter the hordes of expensive New Jersey lobbyists that Trump and company had hired to oppose us. I figured if we were lucky they'd all cancel each other out.

That would leave me, Victor, Bruce and the few people I could truly count on free to figure out how to solve our fundamental problem: in order to build the new hotel, a whole series of local and state resolutions and bills had to be passed. Among other hurdles, we had to get approval from Atlantic City to build the tunnel—a tunnel that was currently "dead"; then approval from the governor, then both houses of the legislature, tap the state transportation fund to the tune of $330 million to finance the tunnel (which included the project's soft costs, such as design, engineering, and legal fees, as well as the cost of borrowing money), and start building the damn thing. Each of these steps would be an uphill battle—and failure at any step along the way would likely collapse the entire project at my feet.

With the tunnel having officially gone down 9-0, I was able to operate under the radar and garner some important support. I secured endorsements from the Chamber of Commerce and the Convention and Visitors Bureau; and despite the resistance, I kept making my pitch to the residents.

Matters got so cententious that I hired John Viggiano, a former Secret Service agent during the Reagan administration, to be my bodyguard whenever I attended large-scale community meetings. I had encountered some virulent criticism in Connecticut, but it had always remained about the issue. There was a distance between the debate and everyday life that didn't exist in New Jersey.

Despite the threats, the truth was that in Atlantic City's black community there was a silent majority in favor of both the tunnel and the new casino. Many remembered Steve as a good employer, and knew that the addition of thousands of new local jobs could only help themselves and their families. Some black leaders, such as the brave president of the city council, a tiny, eloquent woman

Atlantic City Boardwalk, 1938

(©George Enell/Archive Photos/Getty Images)

Atlantic City Skyline, 1995

(©AP Photo/Mel Evans)

Trump Taj Mahal, Atlantic City
(©Bob Krist/Corbis)

The Borgata, Atlantic City
(©Mel Evans/AP/Corbis)

The Mirage, Las Vegas
(©C. Lyttle/Corbis)

The Bellagio, Las Vegas
(©Richard Klune/Corbis)

Lillian Bryant, right, with her mother in front of their home on Horace Bryant Jr. Drive

(©Ted Thai/Time & Life Pictures/Getty Images)

Stephen A. Wynn

(©Bob Krist/Corbis)

Donald J. Trump

(©Thaddeus Harden/Corbis)

Connecticut Governor John Rowland
(©Bob Child/Pool/Reuters/Corbis)

New Jersey Governor Christine Todd Whitman
(©Ron Sachs/CNP/Corbis)

Connecticut Governor Lowell P. Weicker, Jr.
(©Ted Thai//Time Life Pictures/Getty Images)

New Jersey Governor James E. McGreevey
(©Grant Delin/Corbis)

Atlantic City Mayor James Whelan
(©AP Photo/Mike Derer)

New Jersey State Senator William Gormley
(©AP Photo/Brian Branch-Price)

United States Senator Christopher J. Dodd
(©Alex Wong/Getty Images)

Connecticut State Senator Ernest Newton
(©AP Photo/Bob Child)

Edie Baskin Bronson

Elaine Wynn
(Photo courtesy of
Barbara Kraft)

named Rosalind Norrell-Nance, were firmly on our side. Politicians are either givers or takers. There's the kind that truly see their jobs as public servants and are looking to do the best for the community, and there are others who are glorified shakedown artists. Rosalind was the rare Atlantic City politician that fell into the former category. She didn't ask us for anything more other than that we follow through with our project.

Though it was portrayed as a racial debate, in essence it came down to what was good for several people versus what was good for the city as a whole. No one wanted to come out against his neighbor, but in actuality, there were only a few homeowners—vocal though they were—who were completely against us. My preliminary offers to the Horace Bryant Jr. Drive residents were generous, and four or five of them had quietly told us they were willing to sell.

Actually, they had told this to my associate Victor Cruse. I had given him the unenviable task of being our liaison with the black community. His days were spent arguing our un-P.C. position and being told by powerful black men and women that he was selling out his race for the white man's money. One evening after a meeting he walked back to his new car—a Jaguar I'd leased him as his company vehicle—to discover that someone had keyed "Uncle Tom" on it in big letters. When I came back to the Ventnor house that night he was sitting at the kitchen table crying.

I got a little taste of what he was facing when he took me to a meeting one afternoon with some local black clergymen. I wasn't going to sell these men on the Mirage proposal, but my hope was that they could make the situation more civil.

Victor and I drove into the worst section of town; boarded up houses ran along streets choking on litter. We couldn't find the place where we were to meet with the clerics and drove around until suddenly, in the middle of one of the worst slums I'd ever seen, we spotted a lineup of Lincolns and Cadillacs parked at the curb.

Victor said, "I think we just found the reverends."

Sure enough, that was the spot. As we were walking in I said, "Victor, perhaps it would be best if you meet with them while I wait in the car."

Victor said, "I've already met with them, and they're insisting on meeting with the 'H.W.B.'"

"What's the H.W.B.?"

"Head White Boy. And that's you!"

We entered a dingy upstairs room that resembled the sort of den you might expect to find in the Bada Bing! of Sopranos fame. The walls were knotty pine, real cheap knotty pine, as if we were on a low-budget film set. Everything seemed somewhat removed from reality. I expected reverends to be turned out in simple black frocks with black shirts and white collar, but these guys were dressed more for a red carpet than a religious service. One man was wearing a purple shirt, something Prince might put on if he became a preacher, and another donned a ruffled shirt that seemingly came from a junior prom or a pirate ship. They looked more like impersonators than actual clergymen, and they certainly didn't act with much godly love. I was greeted with neither kindness nor politeness, but derision on par with that which I had faced in the town meetings. It was tantamount to walking into a pack of wolves. These gentlemen of the cloth were as angry as the meanest group of Teamsters I'd ever seen. They were furious at me and everything I stood for, asking questions like, "Who are you to come in and destroy this neighborhood?"

Destroy the neighborhood? This was a city with a 15% unemployment rate. There wasn't much to destroy. We had to get rid of nine houses; nine houses for thousands of jobs. We weren't going to ruin the neighborhood; we were going to help it.

My argument fell on deaf ears. They kept coming after me. These men were the community leaders—their choice in automobiles showed they were not struggling to make ends meet—and yet they were just as myopic when it came to their neighborhood's future. There wasn't even room for debate; just condemnation. It seemed like they fed off each other, one of them would scream something particularly nasty and another would take it and do him one better.

I had been hit with so many lefts that I was waiting for a right, and at the end of the meeting it came. The reverends shamelessly shifted gear into what-can-you-do-for-me mode. The torrent of epithets built into a familiar request: jobs, the kind where you didn't actually have to show up to work.

Despite having such a low opinion of my proposal, they let me know that if the price was right, I could count on their support. As one of them said to me, "We're on God's team, but we can also be on your team."

These clergymen were no better than the crooked politicians I had encountered over the years. I wanted peace; they just wanted a piece of the pie.

———

The requests the reverends made were similar to those I received when Mirage was trying to build in Hartford and Bridgeport. Sadly, Lowell Weicker hadn't been far off in his harsh appraisal of Connecticut's part-time legislators. It's safe to assume that there weren't many latter-day Jeffersons or Roosevelts hanging around the state capitol grounds during the mid-1990s. First of all, their votes on most pieces of legislation before them often seemed to have little to do with the merits of those bills. It had a lot more to do with *whose* bill it was. When a lobbyist would push a piece of legislation the first thing out of the legislator's mouth was "Whose bill is it?" The lobbyist would then say, "Senator X."

"Senator X?" the legislator would yell. "He screwed me on the XYZ bill. So fuck him and his fucking bill!"

The only way to change this situation was to raise more money for his campaign fund—under the limits of the law of course—than the other side had. The most potent political symbol in Hartford wasn't the donkey or the elephant. It was the upturned palm.

I eventually lost track of how many requests I got for free "familiarization trips" to Las Vegas, complete with free rooms and meals at the Mirage or The Golden Nugget for themselves and their families. These were not fact-finding missions like those granted by the Ethics Committee, it was just out-and-out freeloading. When I told the legislators or their aides that such contributions were illegal, they usually nodded conspiratorially and suggested we get around the rules by giving the rooms to, say, a distant cousin or housekeeper, who would then turn around and—wink, wink—give the rooms back to them. Sorry. Not a chance.

At one point I got a call from a "community leader" who asked for a meeting in my office to discuss something important. I promptly set it up.

The important something this guy wanted to discuss was the possibility of the mayor changing her opinion of gaming in Hartford. To make this happen, he said, all I'd have to do is provide some well-paying jobs for certain community members who were close to the mayor. "Not that they'd actually *work* at these jobs, you understand," he said. Believe me, I understood perfectly and promptly showed him the door.

But for pure naked All-American avarice, the prize goes to a certain clown named Ernest Newton II, the Democratic state representative for Bridgeport. In a private meeting in my office one day he told me what he needed to convince him to support my bill.

"I have an idea," said Ernie.

"What is it?" I said.

"You lend me some money. Cash, of course. Then, I forget to pay you back. How's that?"

I said, "Senator, I can't do that."

To which he replied: "Well, here's what you *can* do. You can get the hell out of my office!"

In 2005, he plead guilty to three felony charges. Newton admitted to taking a five thousand dollar bribe in exchange for helping the director of a nonprofit job-training agency secure a hundred thousand dollar grant. He also admitted that he filed false tax returns and diverted forty thousand dollars in campaign contributions for his personal use during a five-year period. Prosecutors said Newton used the money as his personal piggy bank, writing checks for services that weren't actually performed and then having those checks signed over to him. Sounds plausible to me. He recently did time in a federal penitentiary; now that he's out, he's running for state senator.

———

I had never been tempted to skirt the law, perhaps due to some unconventional lessons. When I was growing up, it was my responsibility to walk to the bakery in our neighborhood every afternoon and buy the following item: one half a loaf of a long rye bread. Without seeds. Sliced. Seventeen cents. One snowy January day I accidentally forgot the "long" part of the order and the baker sold me one half of a round rye. I trudged home through the storm, and when my mother opened the bag she looked inside and said: "This isn't a long rye. It's a round rye. Take it back!"

I swear on all that's holy that she sent me back out into a blinding snowstorm to get one half of a long rye to replace that awful half round rye I'd brought home. Thank God I hadn't brought one with seeds! That might have really set her off.

When I got back to the Baggish Bakery, I found the owner locking the door. Mr. Baggish was closing early because of the storm. I pleaded with him to open up and trade the bread I had for the one I was supposed to get.

He said: "You're kidding, right?"

"No, sir!" I said, desperate.

Incredulous, he said, "Do you think a long rye tastes any different than a round rye?"

"I don't, but obviously my mother does."

The sympathetic bakery owner offered me a deal: If I'd dig his car out of the snow he'd go back in and slice up a long rye. I dug out the car, he sliced the bread, and once again I trekked home through the blizzard.

I won't repeat what I was muttering under my breath back then, but Mom unintentionally taught me something important. In life there are powerful people, and these people make the rules. Some of the rules may seem weird or illogical, but trying to get around them sometimes means stepping on land mines. I learned to be ambitious, work hard, and eventually earn the right to make my own rules—and to leave the straight and narrow path at my peril.

———

Of course, the level of corruption in Atlantic City was off the charts—even today it seems there's a fresh scandal every week—but paying politicians off was not Mirage's policy, nor were we going to give in to the ludicrous demands of the homeowners. In terms of the total budget for the Atlantic City casino, the money we'd have to spend on the houses was but a fraction of the cost. Throwing an absurd amount of money at the homeowners would have probably made the problem go away quickly. However, that would have put us on a very slippery slope. We didn't need to reinforce the perception—one that was obviously ingrained in some people's minds—that Mirage had bottomless pockets. If we did, who knows how many requests would suspiciously come our way. A promising endeavor could turn into a financial sinkhole in no time.

Still, it was clear that I needed to overpay for the houses. I decided to offer each of the nine Horace Bryant homeowners $200,000—more than twice the market value of their properties.

It was shortly after *that* that Lillian Bryant and her allies launched a "legal defense fund," and it was around this time that we noticed the wardrobe Ms. Bryant wore on her many television news appearances was suddenly more expensive-looking than those of her neighbors. Though it wouldn't surface for a few years, Bryant et al. had a mysterious benefactor: Donald J. Trump.

———

The New Jersey Casino Control Commission forbids meddling with a competitor's business. For this reason, Donald had to be very careful about leaving fingerprints. Still, he ran the most casinos in Atlantic City, so it wasn't realistic to expect that his license would be revoked. While he financially supported Bryant and her cohorts, Donald was also a very vocal opponent. He is a man who will say anything, and this fearlessness is where a lot of his power comes from. There are only a handful of people who have the kind of resources that he does, and there isn't an individual walking this planet who can back up those resources with such an unwavering intensity.

Trump can be your best friend or your worst enemy, and most folks would prefer to stay away from anything that might be opposed by him. Steve was one of the few people who would not be intimidated, and Donald was more than happy to bring the fight to him.

Trump's first barrage concerned our application to be partially reimbursed for the complicated, messy job of cleaning out all the toxic waste from the H-Tract property. When you try to sell a car, you don't peddle an old, beat up vehicle; you invest a little money, repair it, and get a much better return. There were sites throughout New Jersey, like the H-Tract, that were fixer-uppers and not very appealing to developers. Senator Gormley proposed a bill that would allow companies to recoup some of the money they would spend turning dumps into decent land. The H-Tract had been an advertisement for futility; it had sat there doing nothing but eroding the environment. Had it been developed, it could have brought in quite a bit of money in taxes for the government. Though Mirage purchased it for $1, in effect, it was like buying the land for around $40 million—the cost of cleaning it up.

Gormley's bill didn't pertain exclusively to the H-Tract. Our project may have inspired the idea, but the legislation applied throughout the state. The money was available through a fund accessible to anyone in New Jersey that was building on a toxic waste site, but that didn't matter to Donald.

He accused Senator Gormley of everything short of treason: "I don't understand why my good friend the senator is offering so much of the taxpayers' money to somebody who was willing to come to town without it."[1] But Mirage wasn't willing to come to town if the situation wasn't right, and Donald knew it.

Meanwhile, Roger Wagner, one of Trump's executives in Atlantic City, was threatening to have the Casino Association of New Jersey (of which Wagner was chairman) pull out of the

Greater Atlantic City Chamber of Commerce because of its support of the bill.

After I spent a week in Trenton lobbying the passage of Gormley's bill and less than 24 hours after the Senate Natural Resources and Economic Development Committee unanimously approved it, Trump was trashing the legislation on a local radio talk show and urging the news media to "investigate" why Gormley would back such a measure.

What Donald seems to have forgotten is that the city had put the H-tract up for sale years ago. It had gotten no interest whatsoever. It had been less than a year since he proposed his golf course—a proposal accompanied by a bid of zero dollars. He didn't complain about the "giveaway" when he was vying for the property, but all that seemed irrelevant to Trump, who said: "This is one of the greatest wastes of public money I've ever seen." [2]

————

Trump had a powerful ally in Arthur Goldberg. Goldberg was in his mid-fifties, a New Jersey native who was wired into law enforcement and the Democratic Party. This tough, nasty executive had a serious cop fetish and was always flashing honorary police badges and throwing benefits for police benevolent associations. In his home state he was a big wheel among Democrats, a major fundraiser who could always be seen clinging to people such as former Governor Brendan Byrne and then-Vice President Al Gore. He didn't get nearly as much publicity as Donald but, working mostly behind the scenes, he was lethal. He was happy to make the snowballs, put rocks in them and then hand them to Donald to throw.

Trump, in many ways, is a lot like Muhammad Ali. "The Greatest" was the undisputed king of trash talking, and while his comments about fighters like Joe Frazier seemed to have nothing to do with boxing, they weren't delivered out of malice—they were psychological ploys that had the added bonus of building up the gate. When Donald insulted Steve, it was business, but when Arthur had something to say, it was personal. Goldberg was jealous of Steve's fame and success and clearly didn't want him in town. He was the CEO of Bally's, which owned two hotel-casinos—The Grand (formerly Steve's Golden Nugget) and Park Place—in Atlantic City. He was a rough, tough businessman who started out in his family's New Jersey trucking business, made it a much bigger New Jersey trucking business, bought up lots of stock in Bally's, a failing corporation, and turned the company around by selling off unprofitable divisions such as fitness centers and pinball machines and concentrating on gaming. He also was pretty good at keeping potential competitors stuck in quicksand.

A Jersey guy, he was angered by the welcome the state gave to Steve, an outsider from Las Vegas. This was his turf, and he saw the local politicians and business leaders deferring to the out-of-towner. That always bothered Goldberg and he took every opportunity to say so. It was no secret that there was no love lost between Arthur and Steve. One day while at my Connecticut office I received a call from Dr. Elias Ghanem. Ghanem was an internist in Las Vegas who was the primary physician for both Steve Wynn and Arthur Goldberg. I'd met him but couldn't say I really knew him. So I was surprised when my secretary told me he was on the phone.

When I answered he said, "Skip, you may know that I take care of Steve as well as Arthur Goldberg—and I'm troubled by some of the caustic remarks that Steve has made about Arthur."

There was a split second of silence as I tried to make sense of the call. Why would the doctor to both men call me with his concerns? There was a pause and then Goldberg got on the phone. He introduced himself by saying in a loud and very angry voice:

"Listen to me. Wynn has been saying things about me and I want you to give him this message. You tell that blind bastard he had better never utter my name again if he knows what's good for him. To *anyone*."

I quickly responded, "Blind bastard? *Blind bastard?* You fucking low-life piece of scum! You're more pathetic than I ever imagined!" and slammed the phone down.

We had our hands full just trying to get our message across to the community, but with Trump and Goldberg entering the fray, we now knew we had to fight a battle on two fronts. If they wanted it to get ugly, well, it was going to get ugly.

CHAPTER 7

The 4th of July
Massacre

WHILE HE MAY be forever remembered for his inappropriate comments about the Rutgers women's basketball team, Don Imus used to host one of the most influential radio programs in the country. So when Steve, who is never shy about rising to a challenge, decided to answer Donald's allegations, he put a call into "Imus in the Morning."

"I don't think he likes me. I don't think The Donald likes me. I've tried so hard. And it doesn't work," Steve said in mock disappointment as he feigned tears. He attacked Trump in an area where Donald was vulnerable—the financial state of his casinos: "No one has ever equaled his record. Three failures. Three bankruptcies. No one's ever done that in the gaming business." While Trump had offered many noble reasons for his protests, Steve succinctly summed up Donald's true motivation, "Maybe he doesn't want us to come to Atlantic City."

The interview was a good morale boost for our side—and helped assuage the pain of all the anonymous threatening phone calls and letters that were obviously coming from the Trump side. However, Steve was busy in Las Vegas. He had several casinos to look after out west, as well as the construction of the Bellagio and the Beau Rivage in Biloxi, Mississippi. Donald, on the other hand, was just up the turnpike and seemed to have all the time in the world to put obstacles in our path. Every move Mirage made, Donald was waiting to answer.

I learned this when I hit the road, trying to sell Steve, Mirage, our new jobs and our master plan to anybody in the Garden State who would listen. I made my way through every city, every borough, every township, every Rotary Club, every Chamber of Commerce, every gated community, every economically challenged area in the state of New Jersey. I met with what seemed like every mayor, every congressman, every city council president, every assemblyman, every state senator, every selectman, and every union leader. It was similar to what I had done in Connecticut, but New Jersey is about 50% bigger, has more than twice as many people, and I was much less familiar with the area and the people.

Keeping the governor's support was critical. I studied Whitman's public schedule like the Talmud, trying to match mine with hers and figure out how to "accidentally" bump into her to say a quick friendly hello at a factory opening or highway on-ramp ribbon cutting or oral surgeons' convention—she must have thought I was Zelig. I was everywhere, but I was not alone. The enemy was always at my six o'clock position. I cannot tell you how many times I would leave an office or an editorial board at a newspaper and either Trump or Goldberg or one of their key operatives would literally go in right after me.

Often Tim Wilmott, president of Harrah's Atlantic City, would accompany me to meet with various newspaper executives. I wanted his presence as an indicator that Mirage would not be the only beneficiary of the tunnel because Harrah's Marina Hotel was next door to the H-Tract and would also benefit from the access the tunnel would provide.

Steve was getting frustrated by Trump's massive negative campaign. He called me up and said, "Skip, I really need to talk to you. I'm uncomfortable with the way this is going."

There was a note of resignation in his voice, and I had a feeling of what was coming next, so at my first opportunity, I flew to Las Vegas to meet with Steve at the Mirage.

Walking into Steve's office was not like visiting most CEOs. The room featured two walls that were floor to ceiling windows. The office looked out onto beautiful trees, and the effect was that of being in a garden. The two other walls featured a rotation of some of the world's most prized art. One trip there might be a Cezanne and a Picasso, the next a Matisse and a Monet.

Steve was never alone in the office. He always had his dogs by his side—German shepherds as well as a lapdog—and he seemed to be constantly meeting with an employee or entertaining a guest. Whenever I came in, there'd invariably be someone sitting on the couch. On this occasion, Steve was with the casino host Charlie Meyerson.

I took a seat and Steve got right down to business, "Skip, listen. In life you need to choose your battles wisely, and maybe this one in Atlantic City just isn't worth it."

My heart sank. I was used to Steve being vocal and upset. On any given day he could have been ready to pull the plug on one of our projects. But this was different. There was no yelling, just the look of a man that had come to terms with his decision. Trump's tactics had spurred him on, but at the same time, Steve hadn't lost his business perspective, and he wasn't so stubborn as to lead the company on a quixotic charge just to win a media war.

I thought the project was worth salvaging. It was rough, and it was going to get a whole lot rougher, but I knew the payoff would be huge.

I said, "Steve, you don't have to be involved. Let me handle this. I'll get the job done, and if I don't, I'll take full responsibility."

Now in a lot of situations, saying you'll take full-responsibility is an empty promise. But Steve is the kind of man who will hold you to your word. If you take responsibility and fuck up, there will be consequences.

Steve looked over at Charlie, who said, "Steve, when we were in

Atlantic City, we had the smallest joint, but we did the most business. With all that we've learned, think about what we could do now."

A slight smile started to break on Steve's face as he replied, "Charlie, will you take half of Skip's responsibility?" He paused a moment and then looked me straight in the eye, "Let's do this thing."

———

Trump and Goldberg's next offensive was to launch an "investigation" into Mirage's relationship with state officials to see if anything illegal or underhanded had gone down. They hired a former U.S. Attorney in private practice named Herbert J. Stern to dig for dirt on everyone involved, particularly Senator Gormley and me. Stern was no two-timer-chasing P.I.; he had investigated the murder of Malcolm X and gained renown prosecuting corrupt politicians—the book *Tiger in the Court* was written about his accomplishments. However, in this case there was no evidence that an inquiry was warranted; it was a pure fishing expedition. Stern submitted his bill to Trump and Bally's a few months later with a report that said that as far as he and his associates could see, Gormley and those of us on the Mirage team were perfectly clean.

That didn't discourage Donald, who shifted his sights to the Brigantine Connector. The tunnel proposal had been resuscitated, and at every opportunity Trump described it as a "private driveway" built to "Wynn's front door" with public money. Never mind that it opened the H-Tract for development or would decrease traffic jams in Atlantic City as a whole. Donald catalogued his complaints in a letter to Mayor Whelan that was also sent to *The Press*. Trump wrote that the H-Tract development deal would be "the biggest giveaway in the history of government-private sector dealings." [1]

When Mirage made preliminary deals to build joint ventures on the H-Tract with Boyd Gaming and Circus Circus, Donald accused Steve of making money off the "giveaway." Nonsense, said

Steve. Mirage simply wanted to work with other major gaming companies in order to increase development. It was hardly a surprise as Circus Circus had worked with Mirage on our initial proposal for the H-Tract. Three companies working in concert would provide more jobs for the unemployed and greater revenue for the state. The goal wasn't just to build a casino, but to rebuild Atlantic City. The market wasn't saturated and we certainly weren't worried about being outclassed. Steve prided himself on the quality of his projects and was confident that if he had a place in town, you had to see it. The Mirage had around 3,000 rooms, so maximum occupancy was about 6,000. However, there might be as many as 25,000 people in the hotel on any given day. Perhaps they stayed somewhere else, but they ate at the Mirage, took in a show at the Mirage and gambled at the Mirage. The aim was to make "dormitories" out of other hotels, and wherever he went, Steve made that happen. Unlike some companies, we weren't afraid of the competition; we embraced it.

———

The Brigantine Connector depended on the approval of the City Council, and the politicians depended on their constituents. Most of the residents didn't know the ins and outs of the issue, just the sound bites, and Trump knew how to put out a quote. It didn't matter how baseless the accusations or how ridiculous the comments, Trump didn't need to be proven right in order to win. All he had to do was be a nuisance and stall long enough so that the project would no longer be attractive to Mirage and we'd go crawling back to Las Vegas. As long as one tactic worked, it didn't matter if a hundred had failed. Donald's arsenal seemed to be limitless. Be it Arthur Goldberg or Harry Hurley, Trump had a lot of people who could make a lot of noise.

Hurley was the host of one of the most popular morning talk

shows in Atlantic City. He was a bombastic motor mouth with a litany of sources—most of them conveniently unconfirmed. His show was a mixed bag of everything from politics to cooking tips, all tied together by an ambition to be outrageous simply for the sake of being outrageous. He never met a rumor that wasn't worth spreading.

Hurley made it his daily mission to boost Trump and bash Mirage. He repeated Donald's arguments ad nauseum and lambasted Steve, Senator Gormley, Mayor Whelan and me incessantly (in an odd twist, he had a twin brother Don, who was a tunnel supporter and lost an attempt to unseat Gormley). Harry Hurley must have screened his calls to shut out everybody pro-Mirage and featured people such as Lillian Bryant and City Councilman Lorenzo T. Langford. It was a parade of anti-tunnel venom and opprobrium. Then, every once in awhile, he'd cut to a commercial. His proud sponsor? Trump Casinos.

For some morbid reason I sometimes listened to this guy, sitting in my bathrobe in the kitchen in that musty house in Ventnor while creating our game plan for the day. It gave me a hollow feeling in my stomach and made me want to pick up the radio and throw it across the room in frustration, but I felt compelled to tune in. I credit Victor Cruse for always coming down to breakfast in a good mood and inevitably making me turn off the radio and focus on the task at hand.

Despite all the heat in the media, we were gaining momentum. February had been a good month. I was able to announce that most of the Horace Bryant Jr. homeowners had agreed to the options on their houses and even though the pressure was escalating, the City Council held firm on Mirage's right to develop the H-Tract. I had built a lot of union support and supplemented these endorsements with overwhelming polling data. Aside from a small contingent, Atlantic City wanted the H-Tract developed; the city wanted the jobs we would create. There was enough cover for the politicians to stand up and side with us. Well, most of them.

In March, Councilman Langford called a press conference in

council chambers to make the "helpful" suggestion that, in exchange for the H-Tract, Mirage should give $600 million directly to the city's residents. Cash wasn't absolutely necessary, Langford said generously: "The issuing of stock would indicate a good faith effort." [2]

In six months, a one dollar piece of land was now valued at $600 million? There was a new kind of mathematics at work here, as far as I knew, we hadn't discovered an oil well in the interim. Not only would giving away shares to the residents be unprecedented, but it would remain unique, as such a gesture would have been step one in professional suicide.

Joe Weinert of the Atlantic City *Press* called me for my reaction. I could recognize theater of the absurd when I saw it. "These poor fellows are really misguided," I said. "If they're being coached, they're not really serving the best interests of the residents."

And they weren't acting in their residents' best interest, but was the man on the street more likely to believe his local councilman or a major Las Vegas corporation? If "possession is 9/10ths of the law," then perception is 9/10ths of a political argument. My task was to change the deep-rooted misconceptions Mirage faced, as our opponents were increasingly relying on the tactics of desperation. This didn't mean we were in the clear; to the contrary, this was when we needed to be more cautious than ever. As any boxer will tell you, a hurt fighter is a dangerous fighter.

Periodically, the mayor and other politicians would show up at public meetings and the citizens of Atlantic City would express their opinions on the matter. For these occasions Victor and I would round up our local allies and bus them in from all over South Jersey—including hundreds of union members who would benefit from the Mirage construction project. Donald and Arthur and their helpers would round up all their backers and supplement them with as many homeless people they could entice. When we knew that Trump would have a hundred people to shout me down, we'd get two hundred people of our own to applaud me.

The federal government had created a blue-ribbon task force to evaluate the spread of gaming and its effect on American society. There were ministers, educators and other academicians on the team. The late Terry Lanni, a first class, smart, and even-tempered guy who was the head of MGM Resorts at the time, was the casino industry's representative on the panel.

When I ran into Terry at an event in Las Vegas he told me that the panel was visiting and holding hearings in the major cities where gaming was legal to assess its impact on these communities. He said they were coming to Atlantic City and he was concerned about the "war" that was underway there—and asked whether I could help tone down the rhetoric. I agreed that it was ugly but that Trump and Goldberg were throwing the punches. I was only counterpunching.

The day Terry and the commission arrived in town, they held a community meeting at the Atlantic City Convention Center. When the panel members arrived at the hall they were greeted at the entrance by two busloads of protestors, all holding professionally made placards reading "Save Our Homes," "Mayor Whelan Is A Sell-out," and "You Lose With Wynn."

At the end of the day I saw Terry at the convention center. There was a television in the room, and a local TV news reporter was interviewing one of the protesters who appeared to be homeless. The reporter stuck a microphone in his face and asked, "Why are you here?"

His answer: "I was in my neighborhood when this bus showed up. A man out front said 'If you'll get on the bus and come to a rally you get a sandwich and $20.' So I came. They handed me this sign when we got here."

That was it. The guy had no clue about Steve, Donald, the tunnel controversy, or for that matter much of anything else. I turned to Terry Lanni and said, "I rest my case."

Despite—or maybe because of—stunts like these, the momentum remained with us. At the end of March, there was yet another vote on the H-Tract, and the results were once again in our favor.

A triumphant Steve Wynn, making a rare appearance in Atlantic City, addressed the City Council: "The shortfall in the infrastructure of this community has been one of its great continuing heartaches, and before we began the huge process of creating a whole new destination resort area at the H-Tract, we had to deal with that. And we realized if we did nothing—if we never came before this council to discuss a road, or anything to do with Horace Bryant Drive, or any area in that wonderful neighborhood—that if we built one single hotel, let alone five or six, by the time that Harrah's expanded, that neighborhood was going to be adversely and negatively impacted by the additional traffic.

"And so in order to get people to the H-Tract and to the marina and to Brigantine—because if new people came to live here and new jobs were created, some of them were going to live in Brigantine—we responsibly and with some degree of sensitivity tried to figure out how we can get people in and around here without destroying neighborhoods.

"And the answer that we came up with was a very expensive one, but it said that we, in order to protect the neighborhood for the future, in order to make sure that it stayed a fine neighborhood, we had to drop down, go under the neighborhood and not disturb it, and come back up after we were past that neighborhood.

"Yes, there was a problem with five or six or eight months of construction. But we said if we spend all that money, that could possibly be done, and if we use great creativity and imagination in figuring out a way to do this excavation and fill it in with parks and green area, that we could interrupt and interfere with these people's lives very minimally. And at the end of the day, they wouldn't be adversely impacted, their neighborhood would be saved; saved not hurt, *protected*, not destroyed."[3]

We were on a roll. State Senator Gormley and my lobbyists got the bill authorizing the toxic cleanup rebate through his committee, though just by a whisker. A special study group analyzing the costs and benefits of spending state money to build the Brigantine Connector submitted its report, recommending to Governor Whitman that she approve it. By June, the newspapers reported that she hadn't yet made up her mind but was "tilting" in favor of approval. Jack Innis was puffed up with pride and strutting like a peacock. He boasted to everyone that it was in the bag, and let them know exactly who he felt was responsible. We had every reason to feel confident, but there was one variable still out there. Whitman would be up for reelection in 1997, and there are no certainties in an election year.

———

On the Friday before the Fourth of July weekend, I was in the Ventnor house getting ready to go back to Connecticut to spend some time with my family when the phone rang. It was Carl Zeitz and Jim Weinstein, two smart guys who headed Riverside Associates, the lobbying company I had retained. "You'd better get to our office in Trenton, because we have the sense that something bad is going down."

I said, "What do you mean?"

They just said, ominously, "You'd better get up here. There are some rumblings going on in the capitol."

I piled into my car with Victor Cruse, drove up to Trenton, and sat in Jim Weinstein's office—which was across the street from the state capitol—waiting for a phone call. Jack Innis was already there, smoking his cigar and looking like his usual, uncomfortable self.

I was told the call was coming from Harriet Derman, Christie Whitman's chief of staff. Derman was a brusque, no-nonsense woman who had a great deal of influence. She was the governor's hatchet woman.

The phone rang. It was Derman. We put her on the speakerphone. There were no preliminaries, no niceties. "Listen," she said, "there's no way that the state is going to pay $330 million to build a private driveway to Steve Wynn's casino."

You never see the one that puts you down. I felt frozen, suspended in the moment. I had worked hard to build political support, but the governor's approval was something that I thought we had from the very beginning.

Then she said, "And if you don't tell us right now that you will split the cost, that you'll pay $165 million for your share of this tunnel, then we are going to issue a press release tonight saying that Governor Whitman no longer supports the idea of a tunnel in Atlantic City. Right now, it's do or die. This is not something for negotiation."

From what Derman told us we knew that Trump and Goldberg's lobbyists must have gotten to the governor's advisors and convinced them that approving the tunnel plan would be a roadblock to her reelection.

Derman again insisted that Mirage pay $165 million or there would be no tunnel. Period. Maybe she thought that Steve had expected this; that he was open to negotiation. I knew differently. The idea of paying for infrastructure was anathema to Steve. It was more than a matter of finances; it was about principle. Had we known going in that Mirage would be expected to co-finance the tunnel, we would have never made it to this point. There wouldn't have been ceaseless debates and arguments with homeowners, there wouldn't have been insults slung over the airwaves and in the papers, because quite simply, Mirage wouldn't entertain the thought of developing the H-Tract. But here we were, a year into the project, and we get the mother of all curveballs.

The bad news would quickly travel back to the Mirage inner circle in Las Vegas where those unsympathetic toward the New Jersey project would gleefully relay Derman's ultimatum. Phoning Steve first was not something I looked forward to, but I had to let him know. Every day in Atlantic City there was a crisis. A councilman would feel some pressure from his constituents and rethink his vote. It would seem like we were in danger of losing our majority, but by the end of the day, it would be resolved, and I'd be ready for the next dilemma du jour. I was running the Atlantic City project and didn't bother Steve with every little development; there was no need to inundate him with minutiae and risk a decision to pull the plug on the operation based on what would prove to be a small inconvenience. But this news, though it had come out of nowhere, was no bump in the road. We were looking at the definitive end of the project.

I begged Derman for a private meeting in her office in an hour. She reluctantly agreed. I called Steve in Las Vegas and told him what I'd heard. He went ballistic. He thought this matter had been settled with the governor months ago. Jack Innis had repeatedly assured him of it. The question had been eminent domain, not financing the tunnel. Or so we had thought. Steve figured he'd been double-crossed.

"Shut it down!" he shouted. "We're out of there! This is the most horrible thing I've ever heard in my life! I don't believe we spent all these millions of dollars and all this time, and now we're—" That was just the opening salvo . . . then he went nuclear. I'll let you imagine the sound and fury. I didn't even try to answer him. I just told him I'd call him back after the meeting with Derman.

We all hustled over to the governor's office. While we were cooling our heels outside waiting for Derman to see us, I turned to Jack and demanded that he tell me exactly what had gone wrong on his end.

He said, eyes shifting frantically, "Ah, this is just a big show. They need to do this. They have to say this. Let me explain this to you, Skip. You really don't know how things happen in New Jersey politics. Here's how it works: They have to say that they demanded that you pay your half of this tunnel. But when you say that you're not going to do it, they're gonna relent. They're gonna back down because they can't afford to antagonize the unions, they can't afford to give up all these jobs that they've heard so much about. You've gotta understand, this is the way the game is played."

To my astonishment, he said all this with a straight face. It actually looked like he believed his own crap.

Harriet Derman, whom I'd never met before, grimly ushered us into her office. We joined her at a conference table with the governor's chief counsel, Rick Mroz, and ten of Whitman's closest aides. The phone rang before we could start. Derman's secretary cracked the conference door open and said to me, "It's Steve Wynn."

I said, "Please tell him I'll call back."

A few seconds later the secretary came back, her face ashen. I can only imagine what Steve had told her.

"It's Steve Wynn," she said.

"I realize that," I said. "Please tell him I'll call him back."

"No, you don't understand," said the woman. "You *have* to take his call."

I picked up the receiver. Now, it's no big secret that Steve tends to be a yeller. He's passionate; an emotional guy. But what's not generally known is that when he's very, *very* angry he speaks so quietly and slowly and precisely that you can hardly hear him. You actually have to say, "What Steve? Say that again?" And he speaks... with... a...cadence ...that is slow...and deliberate...and...that's... when... you...really... have...to...be...concerned.

"Hello, Steve?" I said.

The noise on the line was almost louder than his voice. "Put... me...on...the...speakerphone...please...Skip."

"Steve, uh..."

"Just...put...me...on...the...speakerphone."

I put Steve on the speakerphone, and he went into a full-volume tirade about how we had been misled, that the state had misrepresented, that this was the worst thing he had experienced in all his years as a businessman.

Harriet Derman and the governor's aides were incredulous. They didn't know Steve; they'd never heard anything like this before. They sat and stared at the phone with astonishment and maybe even a little fear. He was furious, but for good reason. Lowering his voice to a whisper he asked, "Is…Jack…Innis…in…the…room?" We had to lean toward the phone to make this out.

In that instant Innis looked terrified. I can't say I felt sorry for him, but close.

"Steve?" he said, in a voice suddenly a few octaves higher, like a mouse's.

"Leave…the…room…now. Get…to…a…phone…and…call me… immediately. You…understand…me?"

"Yes, Steve," Innis squeaked.

"Get…up…out…of…your…chair. Walk…to…the…door…and …leave…the…room…and…call…me…right…now."

Innis stood up and walked out like a man going to the electric chair.

It took a few moments for this to sink in and the real business of the meeting to begin. I didn't see a viable solution, but that didn't mean I was ready to quit. If the Atlantic City project died, all my work for Mirage Resorts would be wasted. I had experienced frustration in Connecticut and I was not prepared to be shut down in New Jersey. But being presented with a $165 million bill is not something you solve in a jiff. I needed more time to think.

So I said, "Harriet, you've got to do one thing for me. Only one thing. Our company has spent an inordinate amount of money. Maybe things were misrepresented to us. Maybe it was a misunderstanding. We can call it whatever we want to call it. But one thing is certain. We've spent millions and millions of dollars trying to get this done. You cannot right now, all of a sudden, at six o'-clock on a Friday night of a Fourth of July weekend, tell me that this thing is absolutely unequivocally dead if we don't agree to something. You can't do that."

I continued: "Even in war, there are rules. You don't bomb hospitals. You don't shoot at lifeboats. There are certain rules. They give you a rulebook when you're in a war. You cannot do this to us right now. You've got to give me the chance—just a chance—to get this worked out."

Unfazed, Harriet said, "Are you going to pay for half the tunnel?"

"I can't tell you what we're gonna do," I said. "All I'm telling you is one thing. If you're a human being, you cannot do this to me. You have to give me a chance. The state offices, everything is closed on Monday because of the holiday. You have to give me until Tuesday. We'll reconvene on Tuesday. And you know what, Harriet? If I can't get this worked out by Tuesday, then *I'll help you* write the press release. And we won't even put anything in there about how we felt that we were abused by the state of New Jersey and we won't say anything caustic about Governor Whitman. I give you my word on that if you'll give me your word that you'll at least give me until Tuesday to try to come up with a solution to this."

And then, while my professional life hung in the balance, Harriet Derman, New Jersey Governor Christine Todd Whitman's all-powerful chief of staff and gatekeeper, thought about it carefully for a moment. She looked me straight in the eye, held my heart in her hand, and squeezed.

"No," she said, and her eyes pointed me toward the door.

CHAPTER 8

The Summer
of Silence

GROWING UP in Connecticut, I often worked as a caddy. One of my favorite loops as a bag toter was for Abraham Ribicoff, Connecticut's former governor and later a U.S. Senator. Ribicoff was well known in Washington for going out on a limb for the things he believed in regardless of the consequences. He enjoyed golf and whenever he played at Tumble Brook Country Club he would ask if I was available. He and his friend, A.I. "Butch" Savin, were two of the most competitive men I'd ever met. After his tenure as governor, Ribicoff went on to become secretary of Health, Education and Welfare under President John F. Kennedy and later became a U.S. Senator from Connecticut. He held as many important titles as any contemporary American public figure.

Savin was a highly respected businessman and one of the richest Jews in Hartford. He was all of five-foot-six, but not one to mess with. He had a big wallet and an even bigger temper. When Savin was playing you literally had to hold your breath when it was his shot. He once berated a caddy who sneezed as

Savin was walking to his ball—not hitting it, mind you, just walking toward it.

I loved it when he'd hit a bad shot, then look around, furious, to find someone to blame. I think I enjoyed it more than the senator when he beat Old Man Savin. Butch played golf at least three or four times a week, and it used to drive him crazy that the senator, who only played about once a month, almost always won. One thing was certain; Abe Ribicoff never had a bad lie when I was on his bag.

Years later, when I was an up-and-coming young Jewish businessman in Hartford, Butch's son Peter Savin was king at Tumble Brook. Whoever the titular club president was, Savin actually ran the place. In his early forties, he controlled his family's road-building business, owned a minor league football team, the Hartford Knights, and was master of all he surveyed—top dog, Alpha male—at TBCC. If you angered or annoyed him, or even sucked up too him too obsequiously, you did so at your peril. If Savin wanted you in his club, you were in. If Savin wanted you out, you were out. Woe to anyone who crossed this guy. Play a little too slowly in the foursome ahead of him and expect a Titleist fired in the general direction of your head, followed by some colorful language from the tee box behind you and a dressing down in the locker room afterward.

I usually avoided Savin. That strategy fell apart one day when my cousin Bob and I entered the club's annual member-member tournament. Bob and I drew Savin and his good friend Sam Blumenthal—an unpleasant stockbroker who also had plenty of pull at the club—as our opponents in the first round. Both Savin and Blumenthal were very good golfers. Neither of them knew Bob nor me from a hole in the wall. The anonymity was fine by me, and it lasted until we were walking to the fifth tee.

Bob, who was nervous and playing poorly, came over to me and said, "I can't believe this guy."

"Who?" I said.

"Savin!" Bob said.

"Why?"

"Because every time I go to hit my drive he either jingles some coins in his pocket or he starts to step off the tee, so that I see that at the top of my backswing. That's why I'm hitting these bad drives, because he's getting me totally unsettled."

"Really?" I said.

"Yeah, you just watch," Bob said.

So over the next couple holes, I watched. And that's exactly what was happening. Every time Bob got up to hit a drive, Peter Savin did something distracting, making noise or moving just enough in Bob's peripheral vision so that it threw him off. And it was pretty obvious that it was intentional.

By the time we were walking to the eleventh tee, Bob was steaming. He said to me, "If this sonofabitch does this one more time I'm gonna have to say something."

And I said, "You know, Cuz, I don't know if that would be a good idea."

"I don't care," Bob replied.

Bob was the bigger guy of the two of us; a trucking company guy, a man who wouldn't be bossed around. When we were kids, he was the guy I'd want on my side if I was going to be in a fight.

We walked up to the tee and Savin and Blumenthal hit their drives. Then I got up to hit my drive. Finally, Bob teed off. While he was at the top of his backswing Savin jiggled something in his pocket, just loud enough to make a noise. Bob hit a total shank, practically sideways, into the trees.

I looked at Savin and said: "You know something? You really ought not to be doing that."

Everything came to a dead stop.

Savin hadn't said a word to me all morning. He glared at me fiercely, and said, "What do you mean? Do *what?*"

I said, "You *know* what. Every time Bob goes to hit a drive, you either move your feet or you jiggle the change in your pocket. Frankly, this is bullshit."

That didn't go down well with Savin. "What the *fuck* are you talking about?" Then he looked at my cousin Bob and said, "Did I do anything to upset your tee shot?"

Bob looked at him and said meekly, "No. Nothing."

I was flabbergasted. Savin looked at me and said, "What the hell are you talking about? Even your partner says I didn't do anything. What, are you looking to cause trouble here?"

I said to him, "That's bullshit and you know it. It's not the first time you did it, and I don't care if he's afraid to say anything to you or not. The fact is, you did it and you know you did it."

Then he stormed away, and I stormed away, and I walked over to Bob and said, "Cuz, what are you, kidding me? What was that about?"

And he said, "Hey, I didn't want to say anything to him. I don't wanna be thrown out of the club."

Unbelievable. I was seething at everyone at that point. We walked down the fairway, and as I was about to hit my next shot, my hands were literally shaking. I somehow managed to hit the ball, get it across a pond and up to the front of the green. Bob was so nervous that he totally shanked his next ball without any help at all from Savin.

Up on the green, Savin was still glaring at me. I do mean glaring at me. Shooting daggers. This is a guy who's part of the most powerful and richest Jewish family in town. My livelihood—not just my country club membership—depended largely on personal connections within the community, and Savin was staring at me like he'd like to kill me. We walked off the green, proceeded to the next tee, and he came over to me looking like he was about to wrap his putter around my neck.

I braced myself for what was sure to be my first physical altercation since high school. He stepped in front of me, leaned forward so his face was just a few inches from mine, and said under his breath, "Your cousin's a pussy."

And that was that. Nothing more. Nothing less. No more nonsense on anybody's backswing. We finished the match, shook hands, and went home. From that day forward Peter Savin and I had an incredible relationship. He'd go out of his way to come over to me, talk to me, invite me to sit with him at lunch, play golf with him and ultimately put me up as a member of the club's board of directors—eventually I became the president. It wasn't until years afterward that he'd ever acknowledge my cousin Bob. Never mentioned him nor even returned his greeting.

———

Sometimes you have to challenge bullies, at other moments you have to appeal to the goodwill of friends, but whatever the situation calls for, you have to know when it's time to make your stand. As I sat there in the governor's office—the meeting clearly over as far as Harriet Derman was concerned—I realized I was down to my last shot. I knew perfectly well that failure—and the triumph of the people trying to stop us, Donald Trump and Arthur Goldberg; and the end of the whole Atlantic City project, and my reinvention as a casino resort developer—was at hand. I simply refused to leave the office without an extension. I kept asking Derman for more time, pleading with her to give me a few days to make everything right, and whether it was because I was able to reach her or she just wanted to get rid of me, she finally agreed to give me until the following Tuesday.

I got out of there before she could change her mind. I was drained; physically and emotionally spent. I got in my car with Victor, and he drove us back to Connecticut for the holiday weekend. We were in no mood to celebrate.

I was mush at that point. In fact, it was such a brutal situation; I can't even give it context. It was awful. Victor was just watching all this, but he too was spent. As I looked out the window, the polluted sky seemed heavier and more oppressive than usual, the oil refineries even more forbidding as they emptied their fumes into the desolation. My stomach turned with the uneasy feeling that treads the line between anxiety and illness while my mind throbbed with the knowledge that I had to do something and the uncertainty that there was anything to be done. I'd used every personal communication skill in my DNA, every last wit about me to get this extension, because the guillotine was ready to drop. While I had my suspicions, I never learned for certain why Rowland had turned on us in Connecticut. In this case, it was a bit clearer (although no less surprising) why the governor's support seemed to dissipate. Whitman, with her upcoming reelection contest, couldn't be seen "giving away" land to Mirage.

At least I had a three-day reprieve. During the holiday weekend, somehow, I'd have to work up a solution to keep our project going. Unfortunately we were at a total impasse. Steve was furious, the governor was furious, and neither was bluffing. Each one was ready to walk away from the deal, it didn't matter that a great deal of money and political capital had already gone into the project. It was a total disaster, and that's when I found out for the first time who our real friends were. I called Innis from the car. No answer. I tried several times during the long drive; he never picked up. Steve called to tell me that Jack never got back to him either. At the moment I felt everyone was against me: the governor as well as the residents of Atlantic City, and I couldn't even find my attorney.

I finally got home about 1 a.m. For the past year, I experienced a tangible apprehension every time I touched foot in Atlantic City, but this dread was balanced by a certain sense of joy and relief that would rush over me on returning from a turbulent week in New Jersey. But as I turned the key in the door, the usual onset of comfort was absent. I was used up, as if there were nothing else left for me to feel. I saw Edie, sitting at the kitchen table, the frustration clearly exhibited on her face. She had had enough too. In addition to being fed up with our long separations during this project, she saw the toll it was taking on me.

"It's never over until it's over," she said, "but when it's over, it's *over*."

She was right, you can't go around chasing ghosts, but I couldn't walk away from this. Everything may come to an end, but the project didn't have to end this way. To be undone by Trump and Goldberg when we had come so close was something I would have regretted for the rest of my life. I felt I owed everyone one last shot.

There was one sliver of optimism to buoy my resolve. My lobbyist Jim Weinstein called and said the state might be willing to pick up two-thirds of the bill, leaving Mirage on the hook for $110 million. I took "might" as a "yes," and though the situation was still bleak—I had a long weekend to come up with $110 million—I saw room for compromise. It wasn't over. Not yet.

The following day Edie and I were going to East Hampton to stay at the home of Martha Stewart. Martha is the exemplar of a Renaissance woman, she cooks, runs businesses, is comfortable in front of the camera (she would eventually do her own version of Trump's *The Apprentice*), and has a knack for finding a use for just about anything. Edie and I had rented a house from Martha shortly after we first got together, and we all ended up becoming close friends. Rarely a week went by that we didn't have dinner, play Scrabble, or take in a movie with Martha. She is one of the most remarkable women either of us had ever met, and she can actually do all the things she talks about on her television program, radio shows, and in her books. She's the real deal, and I gladly obliged when she asked me to be a character witness in a lawsuit in which she successfully sued the *National Enquirer*. However, this weekend was going to be nothing like our usual get-togethers. All I could think about was saving the casino. Before I got on the plane to Martha's house that morning, I called Jack at least two or three times on his cell phone, at his office, and at his home. Not a word; he had disappeared.

Edie was insisting that I at least take the weekend off, but that just wasn't possible. I had precious little time and could ill afford to watch the fireworks as the project went down in flames. I would sneak out of Martha's house to make S.O.S. calls to New Jersey and when Edie wanted to go shopping, I'd walk with her into the store, and then dart out to put in a few calls while she browsed.

I didn't stop pursuing Innis. Having heard a year's worth of his guarantees—assurances that were completely worthless—I was determined to at the very least get an explanation out of him. After my umpteenth call his wife finally answered the phone. When I told her that I needed to speak to Jack, she said he had gone fishing and couldn't be reached. Convenient.

I was in no mood for excuses so I said, "Either you find him, or I'll get someone who will."

A few moments later, my cell phone lit up with a New Jersey number. It was Innis.

"Hey, how are you?" he beamed as if I had called to see what his plans were for the Fourth. "I just caught a 10-pound bass."

"Sure you did. Listen, what the fuck?"

I went off on how badly he had misled us and grilled him on

this mess he had created. Instead of apologizing, he got defensive and cried about how Steve had "abused" him. Abused him? This was a guy who had billed us exorbitantly while failing to do anything more than boast and B.S.

The Hamptons have awful cell phone reception. It's bad now and it was even worse in 1996. The connection was terrible, and though I didn't want to let Innis off the hook now that I was finally speaking with him, I was forced to call him back from a landline.

"Jack, I'm gonna call you back. You'd better pick up the phone."

I went into a phone booth—people still used them frequently as far back as 1996—dialed his number, and Jack did indeed pick up. He went on to lecture me that you have to know when a deal is dead, and he was certain that our proposition was finished. His defeatist attitude was in stark contrast to the opportunistic optimist who seemed to think there wasn't a problem in the world. I kept pressing him to explain how we had possibly reached this point, but he stonewalled me.

"I can't," he said.

"You can't or you won't?" I asked.

"I can't," he repeated. And that was it. I wasn't going to get anything out of him. Innis knew his time with us was up. Nothing he could say would extricate him from the situation he had gotten himself into, so he just stopped trying to spin. When an equivocator runs out of B.S., he turns tail and acts like nothing happened.

I was furious and slammed the phone down so hard that I injured my wrist. (I would have ripped the cord off the phone, but apparently this has been done a few times and there was a metal band keeping it in place.) It was the last time I spoke to Jack, but not the last I heard from him. Innis wouldn't talk to Steve again, but Jack would talk about Steve constantly. The way Jack saw it, he hadn't been fired; he had quit. Just as he had previously given the impression that the Mirage casino was signed, sealed and delivered thanks to him, now he seemed to think that the project was never going to happen. As if I needed any more motivation, I now was dead set on proving him wrong.

After getting no explanation from Jack, I tried State Senator William Gormley. His response to me: "Hey, what are you gonna do? Things happen for a reason. Maybe this just wasn't meant to be. You did all you could."

It was not what I was hoping to hear, but it wasn't a cop out on his part. God knows he put his nuts on the line every day for this project. I think it was just the reaction of an ex-Marine who had been in his share of battles. Follow the Atlantic City papers for a while and see how many of the politicians are constantly getting busted for one form of corruption or another. A straight shooter such as Gormley has to build up a tolerance for deals that went wrong or he'd go absolutely insane.

Gormley reassured me that I had nothing to second-guess myself about. Lawyers often say the best closing arguments are those you make in the car on the way home, but Bill said there was nothing I could've done differently to change the outcome. I appreciated his assessment, but I was looking for more than consolation. In desperation I called Jim Whelan, who was the closest thing to a friend I'd made during the whole escapade. He had told me many times that he was a hundred percent behind our project. Unfortunately, so had Innis.

I said to Whelan, "We've gotta do something. We've got too much at risk. You put your name on the line; we put our company's reputation and money on the line. We have to come up with some sort of compromise. We've gotta make this work. Look, you've got to get to the governor. She's madder than a hornet right now because she thinks she was lied to; apparently she was told that Mirage was always going to pay for at least half of this tunnel.

Of course, Innis told me the state would be picking up the bill. But we can fix this. Are you with me?"

Whelan was up for the fight. At this point we were the only two people who believed an agreement could be reached, and that probably had more to do with wishful thinking than any evidence. But at least I had an ally, someone who could act as an intermediary with the governor. It was up to me to convince Steve, and it was up to Jim to deliver Whitman. Now, please understand the dynamic here. The mayor was a Democrat and the governor was a Republican. The mayor was from South Jersey, and the governor from North Jersey. They were polar opposites in almost every way. Jim Whelan, bless him, said he would do his best for me.

Somehow, some way, on that holiday weekend, Whelan persuaded Governor Whitman, at the time a major force in national politics and even being talked about as a presidential or vice presidential candidate, to take a conference call with Jim and me about the Brigantine Connector. Just as soon as we got the call going, I begged their tolerance, put them all on hold, and called Steve Wynn in Las Vegas. Steve was not in a good mood. Who could blame him?

I said to Steve, quickly, "Let me fill you in. There's going to have to be a compromise. And I'd like to tell you that I can get this resolved. That you're still going to get the tunnel, but the government's not going pay for all of it. That's just not gonna happen."

I kept speaking rapidly to keep him from objecting. "So now that we know that, let's accept that as a given. You can make the decision to say, 'No, we're out of here. Blow this whole thing off.' But then Trump wins. He beats us. All the money we spent is down the drain. Eventually, this whole project is gonna cost hundreds of millions of dollars, perhaps north of a billion dollars to build the first hotel. I'm not telling you that the amount we're likely going to chip in isn't a lot of money. It is. But it's just a fraction of the total. So somehow we're gonna get this thing worked out."

Steve seemed like he was willing to give it one more chance—at the very least, he didn't say he wouldn't. I knew that he liked and admired Jim Whelan, so the mayor would act as a helpful buffer. I also knew he was too smart to lose his temper, be anything less than courteous to a person as important as Christie Whitman. So I conferenced him in.

"Hi, Governor, how are you?"

"Hi, Steve, how are you?"

It was as if there wasn't this major cloud hanging over us. Steve didn't want to offend Whitman and she didn't want to offend him. Still, the casual cordiality felt odd given the circumstances. We were soon joined by Jim Kennedy, the head of the Community Reinvestment Development Authority (CRDA). The casinos paid the CRDA two percent of each casino's gaming wins. Kennedy, a close ally and student of Bill Gormley, was a curmudgeon, an unassuming man (every day seemed to be casual Friday and his office looked like it belonged to a first-year college student), and he spoke with such a soft voice that I usually had trouble hearing what he had to say. However, he was one of the most intelligent people in Atlantic City; a little guy with a big brain. The fact that the governor reached out to him and got him on the conference call was a step in the right direction, and I took this as a sign that there might be a chance of a favorable resolution.

The CDRA funded projects that would improve the image and living conditions in Atlantic City, and Kennedy suggested there were funds available in the CRDA coffers to contribute toward the three hundred and thirty million dollar tunnel. He came up with the idea that the CRDA would put up one hundred and ten million dollars by floating a bond, the state would put up one hundred and ten million, and Mirage Resorts would pay the one hundred and ten million balance toward the building of the tunnel—but that fifty-five million dollars of the bill on Mirage's end would be a credit against future taxes paid to the CRDA, so that the net cost to Mirage Resorts would be fifty-five million dollars.

This sounded like a good compromise to me, except for two problems: the governor didn't want to pay anything, and neither did Steve. I put them all on hold again, and talked privately to Steve. I reiterated that because we were getting the marina property, one hundred-and-fifty usable acres for free, and that we would likely capture most of the business in Atlantic City, a "mere" fifty-five million dollars was not too much to pay.

While I know Steve resented the fact that the state seemed to have reneged on its deal, I'm convinced that the government never agreed to the financial commitment that Jack Innis had represented to us in the first place. I don't think state officials ever intended to pay for the entire tunnel project.

While I was on with Steve, the mayor clearly worked on the governor, because when we all hooked up again we were basically in agreement. After much contention, the parameters of a deal were in place. Once again I thought we were on our way. Everyone was so relieved we were back in business that we didn't bother fretting over the particulars. There was one significant point that had yet to be determined.

———

Projects are either design/build, in which case the architect and contractor collaborate all the way through, or they are "build to suit," meaning the architect hands the contractor the plans, who in turn executes the scheme. For those projects that are build to suit, there are two ways a contractor is selected. Either the developer turns to someone he likes and hires him straight out (like the relationship between a director and an editor, a good collaboration between a contractor and developer will often continue for several projects) or various contractors bid for the job. Since the Brigantine Connector was mostly state financed, the contractor would have to be chosen through a bidding process.

When contractors submit a bid, they have to follow through and complete the construction for that amount. Someone can't bid extremely low (in order to secure the contract) and then turn around and charge a lot more. However, there are "acts of God," unforeseeable and unpreventable events such as storms that can delay construction and add to the cost. There are also changes that are part of the construction process. A plan can seem perfect on paper, but once it's actually implemented, it evolves in unanticipated ways. For example, you might be in the middle of remodeling a house and realize that a half bath needs to be a full bath, the maple should really be oak, and the bay window doesn't work after all. All of these adjustments fall into the category of change orders, and they are the responsibility of the client, not the contractor.

On July 3, the governor announced her approval of the Brigantine Connector; the plan not only included funding from Mirage, but also featured construction that would benefit Boardwalk casinos. The deal was generally greeted as a good compromise and there were sound bites galore from a pleased Jim Whelan to a somewhat placated Donald Trump. However, there was one person who was nowhere to be seen (or heard): Steve Wynn.

When both sides looked at the details they discovered that neither the state nor Mirage was designated as responsible for covering potential cost overruns in building the tunnel and roadway. And there are always cost overruns. The newspapers reported that Mirage would pay these charges, but we had not made such a commitment. Unless one side agreed to pay these fees, the deal was going to fall apart again.

I am a fairly verbose guy, Steve said I "can talk to a dead person," but following the governor's approval of the Brigantine Connector—despite the absence of a signed agreement and one very big question as yet unaddressed—I went into full no comment mode. There's a natural tendency to feel compelled to speak to reporters—a lot of my work is fairly similar to political campaigning and is thus played in the media—but just because a newspaper reporter calls you, it doesn't mean you have to call back. Off the record usually means that it will still get published—just not attributed to you—and with Trump and Goldberg ready to seize on the slightest misstep, I didn't want to give our opponents anything to work with.

July 4, July 5, July 6…The days passed and still no word from Wynn or anyone in the Mirage camp. It would be three weeks before even the vaguest statements were issued. The newspapers speculated wildly that the deal was in big danger. Wildly, but not incorrectly. It would be a shame to have come all this way only to have the deal fall apart due to the overruns, but it was a distinct possibility. And this time there was no wiggle room. Steve and the governor had each gone as far as they would go. The CRDA was already contributing a significant amount of money. It didn't appear there was any place left for the funds to come from.

Frank Wilson, the transportation commissioner of the state of New Jersey, told me, "The state isn't going to pay one dollar more."

I replied, "Steve isn't going to pay one cent more." So, the only way we were going to get something done was to try something that isn't usually done.

During this summer of silence, I worked furiously to find a solution. With the help of Bill Smith, the bookish-looking construction manager who worked for Mirage, I devised a plan, albeit an unconventional one, to solve the dilemma. The responsibility for overruns wouldn't fall on the shoulders of Mirage and it wouldn't be the state's problem either. It would be the burden of the contractor chosen to do the job. This is not the way business operates; it would be like a pro athlete under a team's contract paying for his or her own surgery.

If the state hires a company to build a road for $100 million and it ends up costing $120, it's up to the state to produce the additional $20 million. However, if that same road came in at $80 million, then the government saved twenty percent. Though unheard of, my idea was quite simple: reverse the equation. Have the contractors foot the bill for the overruns, but even this out by letting them keep whatever they saved if the job came in under budget. It would take a confident contractor to agree to such an arrangement, and it would take some heavy lifting politically to convince the government officials to try something new.

First I had to get this idea past Frank Wilson. Behind his back we liked to call him "Hollywood Frank," because he was a big flashy kind of a guy who loved the limelight and saw himself as a larger-than-life character. He was one of the best-dressed government employees you'd ever meet, very dapper. For all his bluster, though, Wilson kept his opinions to himself and played things very close to the vest. I rarely could figure out where he stood on any issue—and when I'd meet with him at his office in Trenton or at his Port Authority office at the World Trade Center in Manhattan, Arthur Goldberg would either be just coming out while I was on my way in, or walking in as I was on my way out.

At this time, too, I was saddled with two attorneys I had inherited from Mirage. Stanley Schlesinger and Tom Malmud were partners in a New York City firm that had done a lot of work for Mirage in the past. Schlesinger was awkward and gangly, and Malmud would often don suspenders as well as a belt, perhaps in order to prevent a possible wardrobe malfunction should one device fail. They were two well-intentioned guys, but they were painfully slow and like a lot of lawyers, they played strictly on defense. Their mantra was "I don't know." I could say something like "I found this great property and it's completely undervalued" and they would shake their heads and shrug, "I don't know." They were the kind of guys who wouldn't want the Venus de Milo because it didn't have arms. Every time I would come up with a solution, they'd manage to come up with a reason why it wouldn't work. Not a good reason, mind you; an outlandish reason that was less probable than the Chicago Cubs winning the World Series the same year a Republican is elected the mayor of San Francisco. This wasn't their legal advice, just armchair quarterbacking. They said the state of New Jersey would never go for my idea and were quick to call Steve's in-house attorney, Bruce Levin, behind my back to tell him so. Here's an irony: at the end of the day Schlesinger and Malmud tried to claim they had come up with the idea of having the contractor pay the overages. But Steve knew better. As the saying goes, "Victory has many fathers, but failure is an orphan."

Finally, despite all their expert "legal help," I convinced Frank Wilson I could get a contractor to cover any cost overages, just as long as the other end of the deal was agreed to and the contractor could keep most of the savings if he got it done for less. I had found a man willing to go through with this unorthodox arrangement: Carl Petrillo, head of a New York state firm, Yonkers Contracting Company, Inc. I had met Carl in the late 1970s; we had hit it off and bumped into each other from time to time at various functions. I knew he was one of the area's largest road builders so I called him with my wacky idea. This very brave man accepted the challenge. But this being a state contract, we couldn't award it to Carl Petrillo outright. I was hoping it would go to him, but we had to put it out to bid, a process that would take many months to complete. Still, the idea had found at least one taker, so I knew it was possible.

The financing finally sorted out, Mirage, after over two

months of almost total silence, formally agreed to the proposal. The major obstacles were in our rearview mirror and it seemed like we could finally get down to the business of building and running the casino.

But Donald Trump wasn't ready to stop fighting. He was just getting warmed up.

CHAPTER 9

March of the Suits

THERE WAS NO TIME to enjoy escaping the summer with the project still intact. No sooner had Mirage reached an agreement with the state of New Jersey than the familiar bellyaching of Trump and Goldberg flared up once again. Their next move—a stupid one, as it turned out—was to try to derail Gormley's bill that would offer Mirage the opportunity to be compensated 75% of the cost of cleaning up the H-Tract. The bill had made it past the state senate earlier in the year and now it just needed to meet the approval of the state assembly.

Obviously the Mirage camp was firmly in favor of the measure, but we were not alone. Politically the bill was attractive because it would encourage new development throughout the state. It was also supported by environmentalists, as it would encourage cleaning up toxic waste. A win-win-win situation. It could've even helped Trump and Goldberg, should they have decided to build on a former dump. Of course, they still saw Wynn as too big of a threat so they commissioned a couple of incendiary radio ads in an attempt to turn the public against the bill. As described by *The Press*:

"Did you see what Sen. Bill Gormley is up to now? More corporate welfare for Steve Wynn," a voice in the ad says.

The ad notes that Atlantic City gave Wynn his casino site, which the ad says is worth $150 million, for free. Wynn also wants to have taxpayers foot the bill for the clean up of the site, the ad says.

The Trump-Goldberg ad appears to take a shot at Gov. Christie Whitman and the Republican Legislature's cuts in school funding, saying: "You're kidding. They haven't paid for our schools…. But now they want to give money to Steve Wynn? That takes corporate welfare to a new height." [1]

This wasn't a struggling not-for-profit company complaining about "corporate welfare," it was the two biggest casino operators in town. I called a good friend, Lew Eisenberg, a very successful fund manager and one of Governor Whitman's best friends and advisors. There's no one better. No one. I asked him to speak to her as a behind-the-scenes strategist and explain that this was just another anti-competitive gambit, the latest attempt to keep Mirage out of Atlantic City.

Mike Shevell, whose daughter went on to marry Sir Paul McCartney, was also a great source of information. Shevell owned New England Motor Freight, and because he was in Arthur Goldberg's industry, he knew a lot about Goldberg and his quirks.

Despite the bold claims, the commercials failed to generate public indignation. As the newspapers reported a few days later, state legislators received virtually zero calls about the bill from outraged citizens. However, one outraged citizen named Christine Todd Whitman picked up the phone and made a few calls herself. At her "urging" Trump and Goldberg pulled the ads after they aired for only two days on two New Jersey radio stations.

A local radio employee, Tom Reagan, was stunned, "This is the first time in my 35 years in the (radio) business that this has happened, that the highest official in the state clobbered an ad campaign." [2]

The bill passed handily on September 26, giving the Trump-Goldberg bullies a nice noogie, and it ended up being more than just egg in the face. They had riled the governor, not a good enemy to make, and for good measure I was able to convince three major Atlantic City casinos—The Sands, Caesar's and Harrah's, none of them fans of Trump or Goldberg—to quit the Casino Association of New Jersey, an organization that gives a political outlet to gaming interests. These companies were for Gormley's bill, but Trump and Goldberg, who were outnumbered but still controlled the group as they had the most casinos, ignored the majority and used the association as a platform to oppose the legislation. New Jersey's Casino Association was effectively reduced to Trump and friends. It was on the edge of irrelevance.

———

In 1970 when I first launched my career as a developer, I had energy in the bank and gas in my tank. What I didn't have was the money to actually BUILD the project to be known as Mountain Farms Mall in Hadley, Mass. I met two mortgage brokers, Joe Daly and Doug Oliver. They took me to a little-known bank in a sleepy section of North Carolina. Hardly anyone north of the Mason-Dixon Line had heard of the Wachovia Bank and they had not yet ventured into the Northeast but they liked the project, bought into my vision for it and were willing to give me a construction loan for 80% of the cost. In order to complete my financing needs Joe and Doug then took me to Hackensack to the offices of Jon Hanson, a successful real estate investor. I was, as he reminded me, a "kid" but he took a flyer with me and put up the 20% equity that was the necessary ingredient. He became an incredible mentor, so much so that my son Jon Bronson is named after Jon Hanson. Since he was my go-to guy and a major force in his home state of New Jersey, I paid Jon a visit when I ran up against a block wall in Atlantic City. The strategy Jon helped me with is too lengthy to go into detail, but suffice to say there would not have been a Mountain Farms Mall nor a tunnel in Atlantic City if not for his counsel.

——

The attacks on the project resumed as 1996 became 1997. Having tried everything else in the book, Goldberg took a stab at corporate espionage. E. O'Brien Murray, A.K.A. "Obie," was a member of my team going back to the Hartford days. Basically he was a gofer; when we needed to get feet on the ground or have an event catered, Obie was the guy. He was never a strategist or even in on what the strategy would be. However, Goldberg must have thought this young man was part of the inner circle and hired him to be a double agent. Had I been unaware that this was going on, there still would have been little Obie could have given away; he just wasn't in the loop. But Obie wasn't much of a spy, and it didn't take me long to figure out what was going on and use the situation to my advantage. Victor and I would feed him false information that he would in turn pass along to Goldberg. He had nothing but fabrications to divulge, and it's a wonder Goldberg didn't realize what was happening. At a certain point, however, it just wasn't worth it anymore, so I confronted Obie and he resigned. The next day he formally showed up to work for Goldberg, who didn't keep him on long now that he couldn't supply "inside information."

Then came the March of the suits. In the span of a week,

Mirage and our allies got hit with four lawsuits. If you've ever been sued you know how nerve-wracking an experience it is. It's not only about liability, but also vexation, and winning isn't always worth it. Most litigants in lawsuits huff and puff for a while but eventually settle with the other side. We couldn't take that route. We had to win every suit, hands down—or else the thousands of little pieces of the puzzle wouldn't fit together. It was as if I'd passed through the eye of a hurricane and was now being hit by gale force winds from the opposite direction. March came in like a lion…and it stayed that way.

On March 12, three mayors from northern New Jersey—New Brunswick's James Cahill, Highland Park's H. James Polos and South Plainfield's Daniel Gallagher—filed a suit in Middlesex County. Among their targets was the CRDA, even though the funds the CRDA took in had to go directly to Atlantic City. That same day, two other northern New Jersey politicians, Piscataway Township Mayor Helen Merolla and Middlesex County Freeholder Director Jane Brady (the smaller the job, the bigger the job title in New Jersey government circles), sued Mirage and three state agencies in state Superior Court. They claimed that the money going to the Brigantine Connector was illegally draining funds away from county roads in their part of the state. Never mind that the gaming revenue brought in by Atlantic City often ended up being spent on projects up north.

Donald Trump was not going to be left out of this party. He went after us and seemingly just about everyone else he could think of. Trump Hotels & Casino Resorts sued Mirage; the state Casino Redevelopment Agency; the state Department of Transportation; the New Jersey Transportation Trust Fund Authority and the South Jersey Transportation Authority. The forty-two-page suit, filed on March 14, claimed that Mirage, in developing the H-Tract, was upsetting the fragile environmental balance of

Atlantic City. Now this was quite a claim; Mirage was going to fix up a toxic dump, and yet Donald accused us of harming the environment. The way Trump spun it, our construction was going to poison the water supply. It was fear mongering straight out of a 1950s B-movie. For those that weren't as preoccupied with doomsday scenarios, the suit also claimed that the money the Casino Reinvestment Development Authority had agreed to contribute to the tunnel was about to be given illegally because it drew on funds that should have been spent on programs to benefit the disabled and elderly. Surely that's why Trump was so intent on fighting us tirelessly in court.

Now, how's this for chutzpah? Trump's lawyers filed the lawsuit *one half hour* before his company picked up a $2.3 million check for state-subsidized casino expansion from—you guessed it—the New Jersey Casino Redevelopment Agency! It was classic Donald. Very entertaining. Get this man a network TV show.

A few days later our old friend Lillian Bryant and her handful of Horace Bryant Drive holdouts filed a suit against us. Backed primarily—at least we thought—by the local NAACP and other civic organizations, their lawsuit against Atlantic City had been thrown out of federal court in December 1996. Undaunted, they filed another one against Mirage, the state of New Jersey, and four other state agencies in March 1997.

These four suits arrived in quick succession and the cumulative impact was dizzying. Relief was nowhere in sight, and these suits would hardly be the last of our legal hurdles. We got sued, it seemed, by everyone and anyone out there who'd been unable to stop us by any other means. America's litigious ways are a common punch line, but it's hard to really appreciate how crazy it can get until you are waist deep in legal nightmares. All the suits were frivolous, but that didn't really matter much. When our opponents had their lawsuits tossed out, they filed appeal after appeal, making motions and taking depositions and going "judge shopping" for some eccentric local or state or federal magistrate somewhere, anywhere, who would keep their lawsuit alive. And that's all they needed to do; the clock was on their side.

However, we were far from defenseless in these matters. Two of the New Jersey lawyers I hired, Ed Fitzpatrick and his partner Bob DeCotiis, were geniuses. They were definitely outnumbered, but never unprepared or overwhelmed. DeCotiis was masterful at handling the political aspect of the law and Fitzpatrick was the best litigator I've ever seen. Actually, he hated that label and would say, "I'm not a litigator. A litigator is a guy who writes nasty letters and tries to set up meetings. I'm a trial lawyer. I go to a courthouse and get you justice." A tireless worker, but also a hard drinker and chain smoker, he was about 75 pounds overweight. He'd ask you what size pants you wore and if you replied "34," he'd tell you he wore a 32. Which he did, but not around his waist. His pants were so low his stomach would hang over them. He was quite a character and somehow he managed to be both tenacious and likeable; I had all the confidence in the world that he could lead us on the legal front.

In the meantime, though, there's nothing a bureaucrat or politician hates more than to be in any sort of legal jeopardy. The lawsuits gummed up, slowed down, and often brought to a groaning halt the wheels of regulatory progress. Any delay, of course, was to Trump and Goldberg's advantage. On the heels of Trump's suit, the CRDA delayed the funding of the tunnel.

———

In addition to engaging in a duel to the fiscal death with our enemies, we sometimes had to squabble with our friends. After the July 1996 Whitman-Wynn compromise, the question came up as to whether, for complicated tax reasons I could probably explain in a five-page long footnote but won't, Mirage owed Atlantic City $8 million. This sticking point held up the one-year old renewal of Mirage's basic agreement with the city. The newspapers had a field day speculating that once again the whole jerry-built structure was crumbling.

Our groundbreaking ceremony, already slipping further into the future, fell even more behind schedule; but if push came to shove, Mayor Jim Whelan and I would have gladly split the difference. Of course, there were plenty of other logistical loose ends to tie up. There are a number of permits necessary in any construction, much less that of a casino, and we had yet to obtain all of those that we needed. The most crucial of these was the CAFRA permit (Coastal Area Facility Review Act). In order to get a CAFRA permit, a developer needs to show the design of the project. While Steve had a concept in mind, he didn't have blueprints. Since Mirage had met such vocal opposition in Atlantic City, we didn't want to spend the time or money on a design that might never materialize. As a result, the permit process dragged on much longer than it should have. The lack of a formal design coupled with the removal of the ordinance concerning our deal for the H-Tract made the situation look precarious from an outside perspective. Arthur Goldberg, who was now running the gaming operations for Hilton after they purchased Bally's, thought we were more vulnerable than we really were. So he pounced.

Goldberg faxed a letter to Jim Whelan, and copies to the governor and all the Atlantic City council members, offering to develop the H-Tract himself. The next day, the letter was printed in *The Press*:

Dear Mayor Whelan:

I have read with interest today several newspaper articles which describe Mirage Resorts' request for the withdrawal of an amendment to the City's ordinance relating to the sale of the H-Tract to Mirage. From the information in the news reports, it is obvious that Mirage has not yet filed applications for permits which were required under the original contract and ordinance. Now that Mirage has requested a withdrawal of the most recent amendment, it is obvious that H-Tract development will be long delayed.

As you know, Hilton Hotels has publicly stated its interest in purchasing the H-Tract and proceeding with a substantial development including casino, retail, entertainment and hotel rooms, without the need for public subsidy, free land, and the reimbursement of remediation costs.

Further, Hilton would not require extensive time-consuming, disruptive, and unnecessary tunnels or other roadway improvements in order to proceed with its development of the H-Tract. Therefore, I would like to meet with you, at your earliest convenience, to discuss Hilton's acquisition of the H-Tract in light of Mirage's long delays, inactivity over the last year, and most recent requests for further delays.

Sincerely,

Arthur M. Goldberg[3]

The Press interviewed Goldberg, who claimed all he was really interested in was speeding up development of the H-Tract. Of course it had nothing to do with his personal feud with Steve Wynn. Goldberg's gesture was met with thunderous approval by the likes of Ernest Coursey and of course, Donald Trump. It was like they were resetting the clock to 1995, when the H-Tract was still up for grabs. It had been almost two years since Mirage got the rights to the H-Tract and we had yet to begin construction, but the delay hadn't been due to "inactivity." It was because so much time had to be wasted dealing with all the obstructions that Trump and Goldberg were dishing out. Were it not for their politicking and lawsuits, construction would have been well underway. Had Goldberg been truly concerned about improving Atlantic City, he would have stepped aside and let us focus on our project.

The mayor, interviewed for the same article, said: "We have a deal with Steve Wynn." Adding emphatically, "It's not for sale. We went through a public process where Hilton or Bally's could have submitted a proposal."

Christie Whitman's spokesman, Peter McDonough, said: "As far as we're concerned, we have a binding deal with Mirage Resorts. It's nice of him (Goldberg) to give his thoughts, but it's extraneous at this point."

To have your worst enemy in the world described as "extraneous" by the most powerful politician in New Jersey is not a bad way to start your day. Steve, quite aggravated by Goldberg's latest stunt, put a nice cherry on top when he did an interview in *The Press*: "It's very unfortunate for Atlantic City to be dependent on lightweight, second-string adolescents like Goldberg and Trump."[4] All right, back to business.

Small snags and holdups such as the eight million dollar dispute popped up every month or so, giving my blood pressure a spike. But we worked through it and in April, we convinced eight property owners on Horace Bryant Drive to sell their properties to Mirage for two hundred thousand dollars apiece, about three times the market value. One of the sellers was a plaintiff in the "community's" lawsuit against us. We paid the woman for her property anyway. As my friend Allen Grubman says: "If they say it's not about the money, it's about *the money*."

Lillian Bryant, however, remained a vocal opponent. Nevertheless that month bid packages, featuring the engineers' drawings, went out to three contractors, including Carl Petrillo's Yonkers Contracting, for the Brigantine Connector project.

—

On May 1, Judge Stephen Orlofsky threw Trump's federal lawsuit out of his court. The next day, we unveiled plans for the new casino. It would be dubbed "Le Jardin"—an appropriate choice for the Garden State—and the theme was springtime 24/7, 365 days a year. You could come to Atlantic City in the middle of January, trudging through freezing rain while breathing on your hands to keep warm, but once you stepped into Le Jardin, you would have the ultimate entertainment experience: restaurants, shows, shopping and gaming, all of it encased in a glass palace filled with flowers that were always in bloom. There would be no reason to fly south for the winter, or drive down the road to the Taj Mahal.

Two weeks after coming up empty in federal court, Trump lost in state Superior Court. Judge Richard J. Williams ruled that the CRDA could help fund the Brigantine Connector.

Governor Whitman, who by now was becoming quite irritated with Trump, took the opportunity to give Donald a nice little shot. "We won the CRDA case, so Donald Trump is 0-for-2. I guess 0-for-3 if Marla's leaving him."

It seemed like an occasion to celebrate, but we weren't able to get too comfortable as Trump remained unwilling to drop the matter; he wanted to take his appeal all the way to the New Jersey Supreme Court.

In case we got bored waiting for Trump's suit to be resolved, four senior citizens groups sued the state and the CRDA to stop our project. The lawsuit was filed for free "in the public interest" by the law firm of New Jersey's former Democratic Governor

Brendan Byrne, whose client list not so ironically included Arthur Goldberg.

If Steve was concerned, he certainly wasn't showing it. Mirage's annual shareholders meetings are a bit different than those of your average company. They're held at the Mirage's Siegfried & Roy Theater and are almost always full. A lot of families actually plan vacations around them. Mirage's stock had gone up about 20% each year and the result was a loyal and cordial group of shareholders. During the 1997 meeting, Steve declared, "Outperforming Donald Trump in Atlantic City is child's play."[5] I don't know if it was quite that easy, but I was feeling pretty good. Still, if I had learned anything in New Jersey, it was not to get too comfortable. For all our success in court, we had yet to get anywhere near the beginning of construction on the tunnel, much less the casino.

CHAPTER 10

"Royals" Royce

YOU KNOW the song, "I've Been Everywhere" by Geoff Mack and sung by, among others, Johnny Cash? It goes: "I've been to Reno, Chicago, Fargo, Minnesota, Buffalo, Toronto, Winslow, Sarasota…" and on and on. It's as if Mack decided to fit an entire atlas into four verses. Well, I've actually been to just about all the places in the song. While a decade of my life was consumed with setting up casinos first in Connecticut and subsequently New Jersey, I was simultaneously traveling all over the country.

For every casino that you see, there are many more that were never built. Maybe some never left a developer's imagination, others died while construction had already begun. The business is so volatile—billion dollar-plus investments that can be brought down by what appears to be the slightest of details—that you can't really feel confident until a place is open for business (and then there's the small matter of actually running the joint). It's a burgeoning industry with new markets always on the horizon and you don't want to be the last in line. So, as intensive as it is to work on a project, you always have to keep a lookout for other options. I worked closely with Steve in sussing out possible casino gaming opportunities all over the United States. Part of that responsibility involved working to confound the ambitions of rival casino companies. The 1990s was a decade during which a majority of states were hosting a no-holds-barred fight over the legalization of gaming.

Because of the way geography and Mirage's strategic interests were aligned, I found myself at one time or another boosting gaming in New Jersey, Massachusetts, Connecticut and Rhode Island and—often simultaneously—opposing it in New York, Pennsylvania and Florida. I racked up more than 200 takeoffs and landings a year. I was burning the candle at both ends, and in the middle as well. For the record, Steve Wynn believed that Orlando, with its built-in tourist base and more than a hundred thousand hotel rooms, was the only city that could have actually hurt Las Vegas if it had gotten legalized gaming.

Back during the early days of the Connecticut campaign, I got a call from Steve about, of all things, New Orleans. A guy named Chris Hemmeter, who had built some mega-resorts in Hawaii and whom Steve had befriended, had gotten interested in entering the gaming business down in Louisiana. He needed a gaming-savvy partner in this venture, but he thought—for good reason—that if he teamed up with Steve it would be Steve running the show, not him. So he decided that if he did it with Caesar's, he could still be the big man.

Steve said, "If they're going to do gaming in a place like New Orleans, which is already an enormous tourist destination, we should be part of the mix."

Steve talked to the chairman and the president of Harrah's, Mike Rose and Phil Satre. The three decided to form a joint venture to look into the possibilities. They delegated two men, one from each company, to look the situation over. I was the Mirage representative and my counterpart at Harrah's was their head development person, Colin Reed, who's a Brit. (Colin, who as far as I know is still British, is now the head of Gaylord Entertainment, a huge Nashville-based company that owns, among many other things, Opryland.) Colin had a dry wit, and was an extremely capable man; he could probably run any business you put in front of him. However, he was refined and used to doing business a certain way. Regrettably, I had the unsavory experience of dealing with characters that were not always on the level, but Colin was completely unprepared for what we were about to find in New Orleans.

Colin and I spent the better part of two weeks down there trying to make this happen for our companies. And we both came to the same conclusion: Louisiana, with New Orleans as its spiritual and cultural center, was a completely crooked banana republic that any company with any ethical standards whatsoever should avoid at all costs. It wasn't even a close call.

Other than Darryl Berger, I didn't know anyone in New Orleans. The first person I met with down there was Roger Ogden, a New Orleans-based shopping center developer whom I'd met through the ICSC.

He didn't mince words. "Skip," he said, "you need to understand that this place is corrupt. It's a horrible situation. It's been going on for long before you and I were ever on this earth, and it'll be going on for long after we leave here. That's just the way things happen here."

It was indeed. I can't tell you how many politicians I met with there who recited the "Nawlins mantra"—"That's just the way we do 'bidness' here."

In other words, there were no niceties, no intermediaries. I'd ask them if a gaming industry made sense in New Orleans and they'd ignore the question and ask for things. Like $250,000. I told Ogden that I wasn't naïve; I knew a little about corruption, having seen it myself up in Connecticut. So Roger, who was extremely well connected, kindly consented to introduce me to some important people.

First up was a nearly unbelievable character named Wendell Gauthier. A round-faced, amiable man, Gauthier was the "best friend" of the then-governor of Louisiana, Edwin Edwards. Governor Edwards was very well known in Las Vegas because he was a casino customer and he would travel there often, wagering huge sums of cash. Always cash. He would buy his chips with cash, and if he had anything left at the end of the day he would get paid in cash.

Cash also was very much on the mind of Wendell Gauthier. On a particularly sweltering afternoon, he came over to Roger's house, a huge antebellum mansion, and boasted about the car he'd driven over there, a Rolls-Royce. Only, Gauthier called it a "Royals Royce," as in: "Yeah, I got me a Royals Royce. Come on out here and I'll show it to ya."

So I went out to Roger's driveway, mosquitoes constantly picking at my flesh, and there sat his "Royals Royce." A Rolls-Royce is a beautiful automobile, but I wasn't particularly impressed as it was hardly the first one I'd seen. Only Wendell's car was unusually "accessorized." He opened the trunk and inside were six cardboard boxes, all filled to the brim with U.S. currency. Big bills—hundreds—bundled neatly. Only God knows how much money he was hauling around.

He said to me, "Yeah, I'm on my way to Ba-tone Rouge. I'm gonna be payin' a visit to the governor." Then he said to me, "This is the way things get done around here. We gotta take care of the governor. Then the governor will take good care of us. That's just the way we do bidness."

It's not the way I do business. After two weeks of similar encounters, I phoned Steve in Las Vegas.

"Steve, I'm gonna tell you something. The loser in this competition is going to be whoever gets selected to do this casino. Because this is a bad, bad place, and there's no way to get past the crooks here. You cannot bypass them. I am absolutely convinced of that."

Steve said, "You'll figure a way to go around them."

I said, "You can't go around them."

Steve pressed on. "You can do it if you run a public campaign to circumvent the politicians. First, you go to the newspaper editorial boards."

I met with some guys from the New Orleans *Times-Picayune*, which seemed like an incorruptible and crusading publication, sort of like an alligator hunter working in the Okefenokee Swamp. It was the weirdest thing. All of the newspaper's reporters—their crime writers, city hall reporters, sportswriters, feature writers, society writers, hell, even the film reviewers—were investigative reporters. They had to be.

Even they said my cause was hopeless. I remember distinctly going to the original Café du Monde in the French Market, eating some delicious powdered donuts while listening to a veteran reporter say, "Boy, you just wastin' your time here. If you're not gonna pay off, you're not gonna get anywhere."

I didn't need any more convincing. New Orleans was one of the worst run cities I had ever seen, and as the world tragically saw during the response to Hurricane Katrina, the incompetence extended far beyond business matters.

I called Steve again. "Steve, I'm telling you, be careful what you wish for. There is no way to get this deal without paying off. In the meantime this whole area is being scrutinized. Everybody's under a microscope. We've gotta get out of here."

"You really think so?"

"I don't think so," I said. "I know so. What's going on down here is a bad scene."

He challenged me again. "Is this just because you don't want to be down there?"

"No. I'd be lying to you if I told you I wanna be here, but that has nothing to do with this. The fact is, this is a bad place and it's corrupt, it's evil."

Steve thought about it for a moment. "OK," he said. "If you really mean it, I'll call Mike Rose and Phil Satre and tell them we ought to pull out."

So he called Satre and Rose, but they weren't yet ready to give up. "We're gonna stick it out," said Satre. "It's gonna be such an enormous gaming market that we want to stay with this."

"Well, my guy tells me that this is a bad thing," Steve said. "So we're gonna bail on this. We're not going to pursue it."

At the end of the day Rose and Satre wound up getting the license. The deal making and politicking and god knows what else were unbelievably convoluted. Governor Edwin Edwards and his associates selected Hemmeter as the developer, but Edwards also picked Harrah's as his gaming company. The two opposing bidders were forced into a deal with each other, and it was a shotgun marriage in every sense. After Harrah's was committed, the city and state imposed such an enormous minimum guaranteed tax— more than $100 million a year—that there was no way that the "winners" could ever make enough money to justify their "win."

Hemmeter and Harrah's wound up developing a casino in the heart of downtown. Their place opened up but never met expectations. Chris Hemmeter eventually had to file personal bankruptcy—which was major, since Hemmeter was no fly-by-night operator. He was on the very first Forbes 400 list of the world's richest men, and the first person I'd ever heard of who had his own jet. It was remarkable at the time. Way back then saying that you had a personal jet would be like saying you owned your own railroad line. This proud tycoon wound up going into Chapter 11;

developed prostate cancer; and died broke. As for Governor Edwards, he went to prison and was released in 2011. One of my great accomplishments at Mirage is having kept the company out of the Big Easy. Sometimes, the best deals are those you don't make.

———

After we passed on New Orleans, Tom DeMille, an attorney I knew in Hartford, told me that he had a colleague in their Providence office who had a terrific relationship with then-mayor, Vincent "Buddy" Cianci. Buddy Cianci thought outside the box—and eventually found himself inside one. Not just once, but twice. Cianci was a colorful character who Tom described as being right out of a comic strip. That was putting it mildly. I already knew that Cianci, a native of Providence, had had the distinction of winning the mayor's office in 1974 on an "anti-corruption" platform. During the next ten years, twenty-two of his friends and underlings were sentenced for corruption.

In 1984 Cianci himself resigned after pleading guilty to assault. He'd kidnapped and tortured a local man he thought had been having an affair with his estranged wife, putting out a lit cigarette on the man's hand while two cops held him down. After getting out of prison, Cianci ran for mayor again in 1990—and won. Marion Barry, eat your heart out.

During Cianci's two mayoral terms, Providence had undergone a graft-fueled renaissance. He'd rehabilitated the city's downtown area as well as his bank accounts and those of his associates.

Tom said that Cianci had approached Donald Trump about doing a casino in Providence; that Trump had met with the mayor; and it looked like they might be able to get a casino project approved. Both for business and entertainment reasons, Tom suggested that Steve and I meet with Cianci. Tom arranged a dinner, which was attended by the mayor and his apparently close friend, the noted intellectual Vartan Gregorian, who was at the time the president of Brown University. He'd been the president of the New York Public Library and afterward went on to head the Carnegie Foundation.

We all met at an Italian restaurant on Federal Hill and sat in a private room downstairs. Steve and I gave our usual pitch about the fact that a casino could, as Steve said, "hire a bunch of people, pay a lot of taxes, and draw one heck of a crowd." The mayor was all for this and on top of it all, Vartan and Steve were having a love fest. At the time of our meeting Steve was on the Board of Trustees of the University of Pennsylvania, so the two men had a lot of academic issues to discuss. The better Steve and Vartan hit it off, the more the mayor seemed to like the idea.

Buddy Cianci was totally gung-ho for casino gaming in Providence, but there were a lot of people in Rhode Island against it, if for no other reason than if Cianci was in favor of something many automatically felt the straight-arrow position was to oppose it, whatever it was.

At one point I appeared on a television debate with former U.S. Attorney Lincoln Almond, who later went on to become governor of Rhode Island. No one was more opposed to the idea of legalized gaming than Almond. During the debate he proceeded to rail about the fact that a casino would be "the worst hoax ever perpetrated on the people of Rhode Island" and said that he would do everything in his power to stop us. The rhetoric didn't stop there. He went on to say that he would muster all of his people to be certain that this "plague," as he called it, never "darkened the doorstep of the Ocean State." His final statement was, "I will literally lie down in front of the bulldozers if I have to in order to stop this travesty!"

The moderator then looked over at me and said, "Mr. Bronson, do you have anything to say in response?"

I was sitting with a pencil in my hand. I paused for effect, made a note on a piece of paper, and said, "I'm putting you down as 'doubtful.'"

The moderator cracked up, and to his credit Lincoln Almond laughed good-naturedly as well.

The last laugh, not unexpectedly, was on Buddy Cianci. In 2002, as the result of an FBI operation called "Operation Plunder Dome," the dome being the one topping City Hall, Cianci was convicted of racketeering and sentenced to sixty-four months in prison. He never asked me for a dime. Maybe that was the strangest part of our whole bizarre relationship.

———

We never got a casino in Providence, but I knew from the start that the prospects were dim. Many of the ventures you explore aren't going to work out, but that doesn't mean they're not worthwhile. One of the best memories I had at Mirage came from a trip that was ultimately unsuccessful. For the opening of the Bellagio, Steve had the idea of holding a Grand Prix race through the streets of Las Vegas. Formula One has its headquarters in Europe, so Steve and I flew to Monaco with Paul Anka in order to explore the opportunity.

In Monte Carlo, the three of us set off on a meeting with Prince Albert. Aside from the famous race, Monaco is also known as a gaming haven, so naturally Steve brought up the idea of possible business ventures with Societe des Baines de Mer (SBM), the entity that controlled Monaco's casinos. Prince Albert said that such matters needed to be discussed with his father Prince Rainier, and Steve asked if it might be possible to set up a meeting. When we got back to Hotel de Paris, I got a call from a man with a thick French accent. He was Monsieur LeBeau, Prince Rainier's attaché.

"Monsieur, Prince Rainier would like to have an audience with Mr. Wynn."

"Wonderful," I replied. Steve would be really excited. "When can we meet?"

"The Prince will only meet with Mr. Wynn. Have him in the lobby, in black tie, alone in 30 minutes," came the reply.

It certainly seemed odd, but if that was the prince's protocol, so be it. I went to tell Steve the good news.

"I'll have a private audience with Prince Rainier?" he beamed. "That's great."

"Yes, but you have to be downstairs in black tie in half an hour," I said. At first, Steve balked at the idea of putting on a tuxedo but, fortunately, he had packed one for the trip.

"Okay, but could you try to get me a little bit more time?"

I went back to my room and called the palace.

"Yes, this is Skip Bronson, may I please speak with Mr. LeBeau?"

"I'm sorry, sir, but there's no one here by that name."

"Yes there is, I just spoke to him. He's Prince Rainier's right-hand man." I was put on hold and another man answered the phone, but not the one I had spoken to earlier. This gentleman claimed that *he* was Rainier's right-hand man. I once again asked for Mr. LeBeau.

"There's no one here by that name," he said tersely.

"Well, obviously you're not in the loop," I told him. He didn't react well to that and we called each other "ridiculous" a few times before I hung up.

I went next door and filled Anka in on the weird events that were unfolding, then I went to Steve's room and told him I hadn't been able to buy more time.

I got back to my room, and the phone rang. It was Mr. LeBeau.

"Ten minutes, monsieur, I wanted to make sure everything is in order."

"I just called the palace and no one has ever heard of you."

"Oh you must have spoken with someone low-level," he explained and then he started to laugh. When he finally got control of himself, he said, not a trace of any sort of French accent in his voice, "It's Anka you idiot!"

"What…Paul?"

"Yes, it's me; there's no meeting, that was a joke."

I hung up and went to his room; he was crying he was laughing so hard. I have to admit, he had gotten me pretty good. Aside from being a lauded singer and songwriter, Paul has gained notoriety as a prankster, and I can say that his reputation is well deserved.

"Well, you gotta tell Steve," I said, "He's in his room putting on his tux. He thinks he has a meeting."

"Bullshit, I'm not going to go tell him."

"Paul, you have to tell him."

Paul went to Steve's room; he was on the phone telling Elaine about his private audience. Paul confessed that it was all a joke.

At first, Steve didn't believe him. "Paul, you don't know what you're talking about, Skip set this up…"

"No, it was me."

I hope Paul enjoyed the laugh because Steve wasn't laughing and would barely speak to either of us. Later that evening, we met Prince Rainier on one of those dignitary handshake queues. You're supposed to say a quick hello and keep moving, but Steve started to recount the prank, and the prince was beside himself with laughter.

We didn't end up holding the Grand Prix in Las Vegas—it just wasn't practical to shut down the city's streets for a couple of days—but that afternoon made the whole trip worth it.

—

After the trip to Monaco, it was back to New Jersey and Le Jardin, but there was also business to attend to out west. Even when I wasn't researching new projects in whichever state was toying with the idea of legalized gaming, I had to make numerous trips to Las Vegas to attend to general company business. One day I was at the Mirage Hotel when I got a call from Steve's secretary telling me that former President George H.W. Bush was in town to give a speech to a trade organization, and that Steve and Elaine were going to host him at their home that evening. The other guests were Bruce Willis, who had done us a favor in Connecticut, his then-wife Demi Moore (with very impressive cleavage), Steve Bollenbach, the CEO of Hilton Hotels, and his wife Barbara.

Hilton owned Park Place Gaming, the Goldberg operation that was fighting us in Atlantic City. Technically speaking, Bollenbach was Goldberg's boss, so I knew there was a method to Steve's madness. *Keep your friends close and your enemies closer.* I brought up our many grievances against Goldberg and Bollenbach's response was simply, "That's just Goldberg being Goldberg," as if that justified everything. I clearly wasn't going to get any relief with that situation, but the trip was hardly a waste. During the evening, we arranged a golf game at Shadow Creek for the next morning that included President Bush, Steve, Peter Early (Steve's then son-in-law), and myself.

I was never a big fan of President Bush's politics, but as a golf partner, he was completely down-to-earth, with an infectious smile and a ton of energy. He seems to play more for speed than score, and Steve was content to walk with the president and hit a shot here and there, while Peter and I did our best to play a "normal" game. But as we were walking down the first fairway, President Bush the elder said, "You know, Skip, that Demi Moore has really large breasts."

Taken aback, all I could manage in reply was: "Well, Mr. President, I don't think those are real."

The former president cocked his head, smiled at me, and said: "That's okay."

———

Looking back, it seems incredible that I survived the lifestyle I lived back then. I was literally living out of my suitcase and was figuratively on top of a time bomb for months and years on end. I was spending seven days each month in Las Vegas, and fifteen to twenty of the remaining days hunched in my Ventnor bunker fighting battle after battle. The handful of days left over—two, maybe three weekends if I was lucky—I was in my own home in Connecticut, gazing at my wife and wonderful nine-year-old daughter and wondering why I ever left their side.

My absences definitely put a strain on my young marriage. Edie disliked the long-distance aspect of our relationship intensely, and particularly hated my taking business phone calls during the rare meals I enjoyed with my family.

Fortunately, Edie understood the importance of work and had just enough patience to hang on until the ordeal was over. Not quite as resilient, apparently, was our family dog, a little Maltese named Bopper. My wife holds the tunnel project responsible for fostering an environment that brought out the pooch's worst neuroses. In short, Atlantic City took a toll on all of us, even the dog.

The drive from Atlantic City to Fairfield was five-and-a-half hours—if you were lucky—over some of the most traffic-choked and continually-under-construction so-called highways in North America. Commercial airline service to and from Atlantic City was pitiful, and the trains—well, forget the trains. I know I won't win much sympathy by saying this, but the only practical way to make the trip was to charter private aircraft, which I did; and when you're flying through snowstorms in winter and around thunderstorms in summer, it's not much fun. The airspace over the Northeast is as congested as it gets, and sometimes we were routed all over the map, more than doubling what should have been no more than a 45-minute flight.

Constant travel led to other adventures. I used to fly in either a small Lear 24 or Lear 35, run by an air charter company named Aircraft Charter Group, based at Sikorsky Memorial Airport in Bridgeport. One day I got to the airport and there was no jet to pick me up. I called ACG and they told me that "my" plane was in the hangar unexpectedly for service. I said, "You're kidding me. I've got an important meeting in Atlantic City and I've gotta get there right away!" They said if I was willing to wait a few hours maybe the jet would be ready. I would've missed the meeting, so I made a big mistake and asked if there were any other options.

They called a company based at Stratford Airport and put me in a single-engine propeller plane, a two-seater, that looked like somebody built it from a kit. It was something that a dentist would fly on weekends; a plane to learn to fly in, not a plane to get from one place to another. But I was desperate to get to that meeting, so I climbed in. The thing was so small I didn't even sit next to the pilot. I sat behind him as if I were the radar intercept officer.

I'm not a nervous flyer, but this was awful. The plane had all the acceleration of an old VW bus and took most of the runway to get off the ground. We seemed to be flying pretty well for a little while—until the engine sputtered and began to lose power. My heart did approximately the same thing. Then the pilot, his face green, turned around and looked at me and said, "We're gonna have to put it down. We're gonna have to put it down!"

We began to sputter our way toward the ground, more gliding than flying. Luckily we were over a rural area of north Jersey. I thought, "I swear to God, if he puts this thing down on a golf course, I hope it's a par five."

Fortunately for both of us he spotted empty land in a farmer's field. The pilot guided the failing plane as best he could. We bounced along and rolled to a stop as if it was something that little airplanes did every day. We got out and walked to the main farmhouse on the property. After calling Edie, I gathered my wits and called Victor Cruse on his cell phone. I knew he was in New Jersey, and fortunately he was in his car just an hour away. He turned around, picked me up and drove us to Atlantic City. A flatbed truck picked up the airplane soon afterward. Just like that.

———

Unfortunately, there's also a much darker story to tell. On most of my trips with ACG, the captain was a young man named Pat Hayes, and his copilot was Johan Schwartz. They were not terribly experienced, but seemed competent, and they were great guys. One night I was returning from a Christmas party held at our Atlantic City office. When we landed in Stratford, Pat and Johan handed me a gift. It was a flight jacket with the Aircraft Charter Group logo on it. I loved these two guys—as you would love anyone who had your life in their hands. I must have flown at least seventy-five times with them over the years.

Before leaving the airport, I asked what they were doing for the holidays, and they told me that the next day they were deadheading up to Vermont in the White River Junction area to pick up a family and bring them back to Connecticut.

First thing Tuesday morning I took a Delta flight to Salt Lake City on my way to our home in Sun Valley, where I was going to spend the

Christmas holiday with Edie and my daughter Annabella. During the flight I realized that I had left my gloves and scarf on the jet the night before. At the Salt Lake airport, while waiting for a connecting flight, I called Aircraft Charter Group and asked if they had my articles.

That's when I was told that Pat and Johan had flown that morning to Vermont, but on approach to White River Junction their plane had disappeared from the radar screen. The girl on the phone was weeping, and I was stunned. I couldn't believe my ears. I had just gotten off that plane less than twelve hours earlier.

As soon as I got to Sun Valley I called again to find out if they had been heard from, but they had not. When I got to my house, I went online and found a story saying that the plane must have crashed somewhere on Moose Mountain. Search parties were organized, but were never successful in locating the plane. After a year of searching they finally gave up. It took two years before a group of hunters spotted the wreckage. I was devastated by the loss of those two young lives.

———

After the crash in New Jersey, I decided to retain the services of a consultant named Paul Bray. He was an independent contractor and former Air Force fighter pilot who ran a business that investigated airplane crashes for insurance companies and also audited jet charter companies. He advised me on which charter companies would be the safest to fly with from Bridgeport/Stratford to Atlantic City, and suggested I use another company, this one based in Stratford, known as Flight Services Group. It was more expensive than Aircraft Charter Group—but at that point, who cared? I was always looking to save a buck wherever I could for Mirage; but after my near-death experience, I wasn't about to cut corners when it came to personal safety.

Years later I read an article that Paul Bray, while piloting a small plane with his son-in-law, crashed and died in the explosion. Crazy.

———

After experiencing a crash landing and knowing people that lost their lives in the sky, a lot of folks might take the John Madden approach and opt for life on the bus, but that isn't possible in my line of work. And as terrifying as some of the moments were, I had to learn to put them behind me and move on. I continued to fly constantly between Connecticut, Atlantic City, Las Vegas, and California, where we made a push to join some of the Indian Casinos in the late 90s.

One day I got a phone call from Cindy Mitchum at the Mirage. Cindy was Steve's right-hand assistant and one of the people responsible for managing the schedule of the company's "air force." I was in L.A. with our Gulfstream N721RB. Cindy asked if I would be flying back to Las Vegas that night. I told her I was flying out of Burbank at about 7 p.m. "Perfect," she said, because Siegfried and Roy were in Burbank—they were taking their new white tiger cubs onto Jay Leno's *The Tonight Show*—and they'd be done by then and needed a ride home.

When I arrived in Burbank, the animals and their handlers had already been loaded aboard the plane. The handlers and the cats were sitting in the back, and a couple of their other staff members were sitting at the front of the plane. I took my seat as Siegfried and Roy came aboard with their manager Bernie Yuman. As usual, Roy gave me a hug and a great greeting, while Siegfried looked bewildered, as he had every one of the forty or fifty times we had met previously.

Siegfried went to the back of the plane, and Roy took a seat in the front of the cabin, facing me. As we were getting ready to depart Roy said, "Skip, would you mind switching seats with me? I can't fly facing backwards."

"You can't fly facing backwards?" I asked.

"No. It makes me sick."

"OK, well then why not sit on the couch?"

"I can't fly facing sideways either," Roy said.

Rather than make him uncomfortable, we switched seats. As we were taxiing down the runway, Roy asked me to pull down the window shades. "I can't look out the window. I'm afraid of heights."

I thought to myself, "This guy can put his head in a tiger's mouth, but he can't fly facing backwards or sideways, or look out the window of an airplane?"

While we were airborne, the handlers took the white tiger cubs out of their crates and let me hold one and have my picture taken with it. The cat I was holding was named Montecore—the same white tiger that in 2003 grabbed Roy by the neck and pulled him offstage, partially paralyzing him for the rest of his life.

I think of that sometimes when things seem out of control, and remind myself to enjoy the good times, endure the bad, and above all else, to enjoy the journey.

CHAPTER 11

The Ecology Card

AS WE APPROACHED the one-year anniversary of my nightmare Fourth of July, Trump called a news conference to announce a five million dollar "re-theming" of the Trump Castle Casino; giving it a superficial sprucing and renaming it the Trump Marina Casino.

Trump also used the news conference to predict what the low bid for the Brigantine Connector would be. "I'm hearing that the tunnel is at five hundred million dollars and the reason they're not coming out with the numbers is that everyone's afraid to announce it,"[1] he said.

This was pure genius, in terms of blowing smoke. In less than 30 words, Donald not only implied that we were way over the dollar limit Mirage and New Jersey had agreed upon, but he also blamed a several month delay in the bid opening date—which had been postponed several times—on the basic unfeasibility of our project rather than the reality that his multi-lawsuit delay tactics had put us behind schedule.

But he couldn't stop the clock forever. On July 8, 1997, I went to the state Department of Transportation offices in Trenton to watch the bids being opened. I knew that if no bid came in at or below $220 million—the hard costs of the tunnel—the project was sunk. That was because $110 million of the $330 million would be needed to cover the soft fees (design, administration, etc.), and neither Mirage nor the government was going to put one additional penny in the pot.

Victor, Bruce and I were paralyzed with anticipation. It had come down to this, and after all the work I had put in, the fate of the project was out of my hands. There was nothing I could do but sit, watch and hope the contractors had found a way to make the numbers add up. The first bid opened was for almost $230 million. I got a pain in my stomach. It wasn't the $500 million Trump had speculated it would be, but it might as well have been. That extra $10 million would be a deal breaker. Still, we had two more shots and I gathered myself for the next envelope. The second bid: nearly $330 million. The true meaning of the term "black hole" started to become clear to me. Here we were two years into the project, two 24/7 exhausting, litigious years and after cheating death several times we were about to be undone by contractors unable to adhere to our live-or-die budget. The fighting and politicking had been ceaseless, and now the project appeared to be doomed to an abrupt and unceremonious end.

There was one envelope left: the one from Yonkers Contracting. If this bid didn't improve on its predecessors, the deal was off. There'd be no need to hear those three little words from Steve, "Shut it down!" because I wouldn't have even tried to convince him otherwise. If this didn't work out, I was done. I held my breath as it was unsealed.

$190.6 million. No, it wasn't a mistake, $190.6 million. Miraculously, Carl Petrillo had come in about thirty million less than I had been hoping for. I grabbed Victor and Bruce and high-fived them. The relief was incredible. We had gone from the brink of disaster to being in better shape than we had ever imagined in just a few seconds.

As was usually the case in Atlantic City, by the time the good news registered, there was bad news ready to displace it. One week after Petrillo's bid made the cut, the South Jersey Transportation Authority delayed their approval of the funding. This was no major concern—I knew there were just details to go over—but it was yet another reminder that there was no getting comfortable in Atlantic City.

———

The success of the bidding process didn't put an end to Trump and Goldberg's assault on our plans. The offensive continued, and I had my hands full just trying to keep the project afloat. However, I wasn't going to ignore blatant violations, and I constantly pushed the regulatory agencies to investigate what was going on. At the end of July, as part of the renewal process for Trump Casino's gaming license, the New Jersey Division of Gaming Enforcement issued a 74-page report. Part of that report included something we'd long suspected—that Trump was financing much of the Atlantic City "community's" efforts against us.

The report disclosed that Trump had spent more than half a million dollars on anti-Mirage litigation during the previous fifteen months, including nearly $300,000 specifically for lawsuits against the Brigantine Connector. The most interesting part was that a good portion of that money went to the Neighborhood Preservation Legal Defense Fund. In other words, Trump was bankrolling Lillian Bryant and her friends in their holdout against the tunnel.

The New Jersey gaming regulations clearly stated that "anticompetitive" actions by casino operators were strictly prohibited.

This worried the state Casino Control Commission, which was in charge of renewing or revoking Donald's gaming license. The CCC was concerned that if the commission interpreted the report fairly, they'd have to revoke Trump's licenses and force him to shut down some of the same casinos that helped fund the commission. That could push a large, taxpaying company into bankruptcy, throw thousands of people out of work—and, not incidentally, earn Donald's wrath and lawsuits forever. Here he was giving us the fight of our lives, and that was for what we might do, not what we had done. The Casino Control Commission was in no position to alienate Trump.

I went to Brad Smith, who was chairing the New Jersey Casino Control Commission, and asked, "Look, now we know what's going on, what are you going to do?"

Brad, who looked like Dennis the Menace's father—a real bookish guy straight from the 1950s—replied, "We're going to talk to them."

Talk to them? This was more like parenting than business regulation. "What do you mean *talk to them?*"

"Well, we're going to sit down and have a conversation and…"

"It sounds to me like you're going to ask permission to sanction them."

And that's exactly what it was. The members of the commission did what I expected them to do: they wimped out. Although they were troubled by Trump's actions, they didn't see any specific action that should be taken. While they stated gaming laws ought to be reexamined in the future, there was nothing for them to do in regard to the current situation. This was Triple A prime political bovine excrement.

On one level, I understood completely what was happening. Nobody on our side wanted thousands of people thrown out of work. However, I was still furious. Why should the laws be interpreted with a fine-tooth comb every time we were sued, keeping our opponents' lawsuits alive, putting us constantly on the defensive, and pushing us even more behind schedule? How could Trump and friends get a "do-over" when they had deliberately broken the Casino Control Commission's regulations? I didn't think the Taj Mahal would get shut down, nor did I want that to happen, but I expected the commission to curb the illegal practices that were wasting our time and money. Now that the allegations had been proven but not punished, there was nothing to stop the Trump-Goldberg machine from steamrolling over us. Just a few days after the commission's report was released, Trump was right back in court with new lawsuits aimed at blocking the tunnel.

We filed our own lawsuit a month later; an anti-trust action detailing our accusations against Trump, but even as we did so I felt very little satisfaction. I knew that dragging Trump through the courts over this wouldn't get our destination resort built any faster. We were playing his game.

———

A national wire story that ran in dozens of newspapers on August 27, 1997, was headlined: "**Shovels Poised for Atlantic City, N.J., Tunnel**." It hurts to say how far off the mark those words turned out to be. Mirage had yet to formally take control of the H-Tract, much less begin construction. Suffice it to say that after two years on this project, the game was getting old. And so was I. The suits kept coming, the bureaucratic delays kept piling up, and we kept scoring victories, but had nothing to show for them.

November was the gubernatorial election. Whitman would be facing off against the Democratic challenger Jim McGreevey.

McGreevey had intimated that he would oppose the Mirage project and was prepared to use Whitman's support for it as a campaign issue. However, I met with then State Senator and Woodbridge Township Mayor James McGreevey in my lawyer's office (Bob DeCotiis was a big McGreevey supporter) and the candidate was happy to tell me that he was actually in favor of our project and that other issues came second to economic development. Talk about a guy who'll say the things you want to hear. The only problem was that Edie happened to be with me on this particular day and because she's a passionate environmentalist and an active member of the Natural Resources Defense Council her blood was boiling when McGreevey proudly said, "I personally tanked New Jersey's Brownfields Legislation." Edie had all she could do to keep from strangling him.

While the Brigantine Connector was a controversial issue in July 1996, by the 1997 election, it turned out not to be the political hot potato some had anticipated. At the time, New Jersey had the highest property taxes and highest car insurances rates in the country. McGreevey ran a two-note campaign. Whatever question was asked, he'd find a way to bring the conversation around to these two topics. Simplistic, but also quite brilliant. He came within a hair's breadth of defeating a popular incumbent. Though he lost to Whitman, McGreevey would eventually become the governor of New Jersey. However, what he accomplished in office will always be overshadowed by the way he left it: coming out of the closet and resigning after having an affair with a homeland security advisor.

———

The year 1998 began in typical thrill-a-minute fashion. In January Mirage finally took over the H-Tract, but shortly after New

Year's Day, we canceled our agreements to jointly develop the site with Circus Circus and Boyd Gaming. For its part, Circus Circus had refused to honor its contractual commitment to contribute toward the additional one hundred and ten million dollars in construction costs. Boyd refused to pay part of the added cost and reneged on a complicated land swap deal with us. One of these companies would eventually reconsider. The other wouldn't. One would regret its final decision. The other company is still popping champagne corks over its success and foresight.

Naturally, our project's enemies claimed Circus Circus and Boyd's departures were evidence of Mirage's dishonesty and signaled the eventual death of the whole enterprise. The most eloquent spokesperson for this camp, of course, was Donald Trump. He encapsulated the situation neatly, using as evidence his prognostication that Steve Wynn would fail.

The Atlantic City *Press* reported on Trump's disparaging obsession with my partner: "I told you so! I told you what this scumbag would do. I knew this is exactly what was going to happen. I guess this is why I'm a rich guy," He went on, "Those guys at Boyd and Circus must feel like fools because they allowed their names to be used through this entire process, but they have a great lawsuit against Wynn. But the key to this is, I told you so. That should be the headline of your article."[2] The editor took Trump's suggestion and did in fact go with the headline "'I Told You So!' Trump Says of Mirage Deal."

We had initially planned three casinos on the H-Tract and now we were down to one. That meant fewer rooms and fewer rooms meant fewer jobs. New jobs for the community had been one of our main selling points, so we promptly announced that to make up for the absence of our partners we were doubling the size of our proposed resort from two thousand to four thousand rooms. I wasn't thrilled when Mirage was sued, as I'd anticipated, by Boyd and Circus Circus. But this was just business, not venom. I was fairly certain that these suits would be settled with much less fanfare than our other legal entanglements.

The wild card, as usual, was Trump. In February, seemingly at the end of his legal rope, he played the "ecology card" against us. This was as ridiculous as it sounds. I don't think Donald Trump had ever given a thought to the environment in Atlantic City, though I do have to congratulate him on recycling. The same arguments he had used in his unsuccessful suit of March 1997—the whole line about contaminating the water supply and corroding the Garden State—were now back in force. Even as we were busy cleaning up the largest toxic waste dump in Atlantic City, our enemy was dragging us into the sensitive—and dangerous—area of environmental regulation, trying to mobilize every green activist against us.

I got word from my lobbyists that Trump and Goldberg were preparing to file a claim with the U.S. Department of Environmental Protection. This could prove to be quite a blow to us and not because the agency would find us guilty of some infraction or another. Without ever issuing a ruling, the EPA could require us to submit so many different tests that it could tie us up for years and years. We could end up completely vindicated, but it would have been a pyrrhic victory as the delay would have killed the project. I had to act, and fast.

Carol Browner was director of the Environmental Protection Agency—a position Christie Todd Whitman would later fill—under President Bill Clinton. So I called Democratic U.S. Senator Chris Dodd, a boyhood friend from Connecticut, and said, "I need face time with Carol Browner."

"Why?" Chris asked.

I explained the whole complicated story to him. I told him that I had to get to Browner to explain that Donald Trump and Arthur

Goldberg had not suddenly become environmentalists: that this was just another attempt on their part—a very transparent attempt—to stop our project. It had nothing to do with the environment, and everything to do with their fear of competition.

Emphatic, I said, "Chris, just get me an appointment. Morning, noon or night. I don't care. I can be there on two hours notice."

Chris hesitated. "Let me look into this."

The next day Chris Dodd called me back. I was thrilled when I got the call, because I was ready to sit down with Browner. I needed that meeting, and Chris was my guy. Throughout the years I had come through for him repeatedly and raised a lot of money on his behalf. Compared to that, one little appointment wasn't much to ask.

Chris said, "Skip, listen. I'm not going to get you that appointment with Carol Browner."

I was shocked. "What do you mean? You have to."

"No I'm not gonna do it," he replied.

"You're not listening to me," I said. "You *have* to do it."

Chris wouldn't budge. "*You're* not listening to *me*. I'm not doing it."

"Why?" I asked.

"You're in this big blowout with Goldberg and Trump over this project," he said. "I know there's been a lot of litigation, and I know there's going to be a lot more litigation, and the way things happen in Washington today, particularly after this whole Clinton-Whitewater-Monica Lewinsky thing, everybody is looking over everybody's shoulder at everything that happens.

"In order for me to get you an appointment with her, they're going to have to put on Carol Browner's call sheet that it's me who requested the appointment. These call sheets are all public documents and all subject to subpoena, and frankly, I don't want my name in the middle of something like this. It wouldn't be good for me, and it wouldn't be good for you."

I was flabbergasted. Despondent. Then, finally, furious. I felt like I'd been betrayed by a friend.

But in hindsight I realize Chris Dodd did the right thing. At the very least he treated me honestly. Instead of acting like a typical politician who would have either lied to me by saying "I'm working on it," or "I can't get it done because Carol Browner refuses to take a meeting with you," he told me the truth. I admire that. And looking back, I realize what an ethical and honorable guy he is. Rather than telling me a lie and really screwing me up, Chris allowed me to move on and proceed to Plan B.

I hired Washington law firm Akin Gump Strauss Hauer & Feld. It had a great staff of crack environmental attorneys. I went to Washington, D.C. to brief the team on exactly what was going on in Atlantic City. They made sure our message filtered back to their legal counterparts at the EPA: "You're certainly within your rights to evaluate anything that happens that involves the environment, but we just want to put all this into context and give you the background on why, all of a sudden, Messrs. Goldberg and Trump have suddenly become 'Friends of the Sierra Club.'"

This explanation obviously made sense inside the EPA, because Trump and Goldberg's complaints subsequently got lost in the bureaucratic maze. Eventually our lobbyists gave us the "all clear." One more bullet dodged.

Sadly, my attorney and friend Ed Fitzpatrick wouldn't be around to help me. One day I got a shocking phone call from Bruce Goldman telling me that Ed had suffered a massive heart attack at his home and was dead before he hit the floor. I was astonished and quite shaken up as I had become very close to Ed. On a professional level, he had pitched a shutout for us in every lawsuit. He would be next to impossible to replace.

After Ed died, his partner Bob DeCotiis took over and did a
good job. He was helped by our Atlantic City attorneys, Lee Levine
and his partner, John Donnelly. They were smart, seasoned lawyers
based in Atlantic City. Honest, capable and resourceful guys who
had survived all the craziness and corruption with not even a flesh
wound. But Fitzpatrick left a hole that was never really filled. That
led to some problems in the long run; in the short run it was dis-
heartening that Ed never got to see the fruits of his magnificent
labor. During the first half of 1998, we racked up a court victory
just about every other week based on Ed's work. In stunning succession, Trump and Goldberg's lawsuits and appeals were swatted
away by every judge, appeals panel, and Supreme Court that heard
them at both the state and federal level. And finally, after a
knuckle-whitening, daylong "battle of the hired environmental
experts" before the state Department of Environmental Protection, we were granted the essential coastal permit for the tunnel
project. Slowly, the pieces were falling into place.

In July 1998, Mirage and Boyd Gaming settled our differences.
Boyd hadn't paid anything toward the construction of the Brigantine Connector or our considerable administrative and legal
costs, but we reached an agreement that they would come back on
board and give Mirage a 50% stake in the casino they would
develop on the H-Tract. The Atlantic City deal was back on.

——

There was one major stumbling block left in our path: Lillian
Bryant. She was still unwilling to part with her property, and
though she may have sustained her determination, her leverage
was gone. Her appeals exhausted, her Bryant Drive neighbors relocated, her "community" allies gone on to other causes—and,
most importantly, Trump's financial backing exposed and cut

off—she was left to fight alone, and a general can't wage a battle without any soldiers.

I told Victor that we'd give her one more chance. I said, "Victor, go to her and tell her it's over. It's *over.* There is no negotiating. This is the last offer and it has an expiration date. 48 hours. Yes or no, this is it."

Bryant could have accepted the offer and received much more than her property was worth; or, she could have held on and when her property was condemned (seized, not granted unfit to live in) under eminent domain, she would have received half that amount. Lillian Bryant was stubborn, but she wasn't stupid. Finally, *finally,* she surrendered. She sold us her house for two hundred thousand dollars. That was more than twice what it was worth on the open market, but exactly the same as we paid all of her neighbors.

CHAPTER 12

Against All Odds

THE RIFT that Lillian Bryant had fostered polarized the city. You were for the tunnel or you were against it; no one stood on the sidelines and often the arguments got personal. However, there was one person who remained above the fray: James Crawford, executive director of the South Jersey Transportation Authority. Crawford was an ally of Gormley and Kennedy, but that didn't automatically make him a friend of ours. He was not a man that was going to toe the party line. He looked at each issue individually and always, always played by the rules. He never used the ends to justify the means. Whatever Crawford may have wanted, he didn't want it if it wasn't done according to the book. He endorsed our proposal—actually he had been the one to name it the Brigantine Connector—but only because he believed in it, and if we lost on a technicality, well, thanks for playing, maybe next time.

Crawford was the guy I called up when I wanted to get some billboards for Mirage. If you've ever driven to Las Vegas along I-15, you can't escape the lines of billboards that unofficially welcome you to the city—it's a very important kind of advertising. The same is true is in Atlantic City. I asked Crawford how I would go about getting some new billboards. His answer: "You don't." A maximum had already been reached, so new ones could not be commissioned. However, Crawford said that Donald Trump, whose leases would soon be up for renewal, was often late on his payments and Louis Katz, who owned the billboards, was getting fed up. I approached Katz and told him that if Trump was tardy in renewing his leases, Mirage would gladly take over all of them. Sure enough, Trump didn't take care of business in time and all of his Atlantic City billboards fell into our possession. He was absolutely livid when this happened. Getting what you want is great; getting what you want at the expense of your opponent is better.

I even got an opportunity to throw a sharp jab at Arthur Goldberg. In mid-1998, I leaked through my lobbyists and lawyers—strictly hush-hush—that Mirage was *very* interested in buying the land beneath the Atlantic City High School, a boarded-up city property that had been closed since 1994, a property Goldberg had told people he was going to buy for less than two million dollars. The school was located just off the Boardwalk, across the street from a parcel of land that Mirage still owned, left over from its Golden Nugget days in Atlantic City. If you were the Machiavellian/paranoid type—like Goldberg—you'd have thought that I was sneakily attempting to add the land to our old parcel, which would allow Mirage to build yet another profitable hotel-casino to directly compete with him on the Boardwalk.

In early October I attended the city auction of the high school property. There was only one bid: from Hilton. It was for $5.6 million, many times what the property was actually worth to them. As I sat there on my hands, saying absolutely nothing, it was wonderful to watch the Hilton lawyers when they suddenly realized they'd been suckered into "blocking" me with their outrageously high bid.

In truth, I never had any intention of bidding on the property. Mirage never wanted to build a new Boardwalk hotel. I'd used Goldberg's hate and spite and suspicious mindset against him. I'd made him pay a ridiculous price for a parcel of land that was useless to him, and as a heartwarming bonus I'd also raised about four million dollars—directly from the coffers of my most bitter rival—for Atlantic City's perennially cash-strapped public school system.

———

While my focus was on getting all the necessary work done so that Mirage could begin construction on Le Jardin, Steve was concentrating on the Bellagio. At the time, it was the grandest, most expensive hotel-casino ever built, and its opening had been much anticipated.

The Bellagio is modeled on an Italian villa, and from the enormous lake to the stunning pools and gardens, it was something Las Vegas hadn't seen before. Las Vegas was a place where the food was famously bad, a place that had yet to fully shed its stereotype of being a bit seedy. The Mirage had begun the transformation by popularizing themed casinos, moving the focus of the city to the Strip and making gaming only part of the attraction. Now the Bellagio, with its impressive art collection, shops that rivaled Rodeo Drive and restaurants that matched New York City, had completed the metamorphosis. Today you will find great shopping and fine dining up and down Las Vegas Blvd.; but it's a relatively new development and was all a reaction to what Steve was doing at the Bellagio. There were also subtler though no less important innovations. Unlike the other Las Vegas hotspots, the Bellagio doesn't require a guest to walk through the casino to get to his room. This was no small change as it removed the in-your-face aspect of gaming that turns some people off. Steve had long battled the image of gaming being an unrefined, second-class industry, but with the Bellagio he had established a level of elegance that would displace those old associations. As I sat there listening to Van Cliburn play the piano, I thought to myself, "We have to get this done. We have to do this in Atlantic City." That evening was one of the most spectacular galas I had ever been to.

———

Circus Circus eventually settled with us and officially pulled out of the project. Boyd was back in, Bryant and the others had settled, and though the Trump suits persisted, they had consistently been defeated and we weren't terribly concerned. I suddenly realized that all the "i's" had been dotted, all the "t's" had been crossed, and there was absolutely nothing standing between us and starting construction on the Brigantine Connector. Could that actually be true?

It was.

I was worried that the opposition would come up with a last-minute volley and drop a Hail Mary injunction on us. That's the way it had been going for three years, so there was no reason to believe things would be any different now. As excited as I was about the groundbreaking, I was equally nervous that I'd have to deal with the most desperate of desperation moves.

Nope.

The groundbreaking for the tunnel, on November 4, 1998, was truly a milestone in my life. Putting it together was one of the more enjoyable experiences of my time in New Jersey. I made sure that Steve Wynn, state Senator William Gormley, Mayor James Whelan, and Rosalind Nance, president of the Atlantic City Council, all sat up on the dais. I felt like Herb Brooks, the coach of the U.S. Olympic hockey team that upset the favored Soviet team and went on to win the gold medal in 1980, triggering Al Michaels' unforgettable on-air line: "Do you believe in miracles?"

The governor was the first to speak. She ran down all the pertinent facts and summed up the impact the tunnel would have, "We won't just be seeing a vastly improved traffic flow here in Atlantic City, we'll also be seeing thousands of new jobs and that's what this is really all about." She confidently declared, "This isn't just a high-stakes gamble, this is a sure bet, ladies and gentleman."

She was followed by Mayor Whelan, who recounted his first meeting with Steve Wynn, "First time I met with Steve, back in 1990 when I first became mayor, he told me he would never ever ever ever come to Atlantic City. I think Elaine remembers that meeting. I was a pest, 'cause every year I would go back and we would go out for the conference and every year, one of the never-evers would drop. So it was never ever ever ever, then never ever, then never..." I could relate to the mayor's persistence. There were plenty times when it seemed this day would never come, but the tribulations only made it sweeter now that it had finally arrived.

Mayor Whelan said, "Skip Bronson is one of those very, very deceiving guys. He's very mild-mannered, very quiet spoken, but he's as tough as anybody in this room because when the going got tough—and it did a couple of times—he was there and he was steadfast and he made it happen."

An emotional Rosalind Nance followed the mayor. I was touched when she described me as "a real class-A man." She went on to share her motivation for sticking with us, a story about a woman who approached her at one of the various community meetings concerning the project, "She took my hand into both of her hands and she said, 'Ms. Nance, I know they're making it hard for you. But I want to tell you that I hope nothing will make you change your mind about this project. I used to work for Steve Wynn and I felt like I was part of a family. I work for the other one now and all I can tell you,'" there was a wave of laughter at the veiled reference to Trump, "'is that every day I go in there and just hope I'm going to be able to make it. I'm just holding on till Steve Wynn comes back,' and then her eyes filled with tears as she said to me, 'I have three sons, and by the time that project is done, two of them are going to be ready to go to college.' She said 'Ms. Nance, my children's future may depend on how strong you're going to be.' Every time things got rough, that lady's face came to mind." Nance was overcome. She had been a stalwart throughout the ordeal and it felt really good to see her determination rewarded.

Finally Gormley got up to introduce Steve, "Whether you agree or disagree with him on a particular issue, he's the best at what he does. And that's what's important about today." It was a fitting encapsulation. Plenty of arguments had arisen in the last three years, but none when it came to Mirage's track record.

Steve took the podium and recounted a story from the early days of the project, "At the very beginning, another developer here in town saw that Skip made an appearance at the city council and said, 'Well they're not really serious over at Mirage, if they were, Steve would be here. This is just the B-team'—referring to Mr. Bronson—that remark caused a lot of chuckles back in Las Vegas. We refer to him as the B-team, he and Victor, and then, the other fella got to learn about the B-team and has all but asked me 'how much I would charge him to get the B-team to stop beating him up.'" He concluded his speech by assuring Mayor Whelan and all the rest, "I'll never-ever say never again."

After the speeches, all the notables on the dais went outside to the construction site. They had their pictures taken while digging a clump of dirt and tossing it toward the photographers with the shovels that Victor and I had personally spray-painted with gold paint in the garage of the house in Ventnor. I looked on with Edie, Elaine Wynn, Lori Campor, our local office manager, Marc

Schorr, who was then president of the Mirage, and another un-sung hero, a city councilman by the name of John Schultz. An openly gay man, John was the polar opposite of most of the other members of the council, and not just because of his sexual pref-erence. Schultz (and his significant other Gary Hill) were finan-cially successful, well traveled, and had style. Councilman Schultz was a big picture thinker and was never caught up in the minutiae or the hand-to-hand combat that was Atlantic City politics. He was an independent thinker who could not be persuaded into doing anything just because it made sense politically. He was a great behind-the-scenes strategist.

I was both proud and completely exhausted. Getting that tun-nel underway was probably my greatest accomplishment as a busi-nessman—far more significant than the groundbreaking for CityPlace or any of my other real estate ventures. I knew that mak-ing the Brigantine Connector a reality would be a credential that would stay with me—and I would treasure—for the rest of my life.

Years later I visited Atlantic City and drove through the tunnel. It was surreal. The tunnel portion itself is only about a half mile long (the rest is a roadway above ground), and as you go through it, it's difficult to remember how the city functioned without it. It just makes so much sense. But as popular as it is today, I certainly remember the struggles in building it. If they made odds in Las Vegas on things of this nature, I can truly say the chances of this project ever coming to fruition would have been no better than one in a hundred.

———

With the construction of the tunnel underway, I was free to focus most of my energies on other projects, in particular, possible joint ventures with Indians in California. It was now up to Steve, who had a site plan but not a full design, to begin the process of formally creating Le Jardin.

My specialty was laying the groundwork for Mirage endeavors, so though Le Jardin was still a few years from being fully realized, it was important for me to concentrate on California. The tribes were lining up support for a ballot initiative, known as Proposition 5, which would allow them to open full-blown casinos in their state. Historically, a number of tribes in California had been operating illegally, running insignificant casinos with no slot machines, only table games, in mostly nondescript structures in out-of-the-way locations. This was known as "gray gaming."

Successive state governments had looked the other way, figuring it was better to leave the Native Americans alone rather than start a war with the poor folks from whom they'd stolen the most prosperous state in the Union. Then-California Governor Gray Davis, however, was a hundred percent behind Proposition 5. One reason: The Indians by then had figured out that making political contributions was an efficient way to ingratiate themselves with elected officials. Such as Gray Davis, for instance.

What Proposition 5 portended was (1) a massive expansion of casinos throughout California; (2) a big increase in the amount of political donations to pro-Indian legislators; and (3) a lot of new reasons for Californians to forget about crossing the border to Las Vegas.

When it looked like the referendum would pass, a number of casino operators in Las Vegas banded together and raised a tremendous pool of money to campaign against the approval of Proposition 5. Mirage Resorts was one of them. When it became apparent that the proposition would likely pass, a number of opponents filed a lawsuit claiming that it was unconstitutional. As a result, Proposition 5 was overturned even before the vote. Shortly thereafter the Indians modified the one clause in Proposition 5 that was found legally deficient and came back in force with a new initiative known as Proposition 1A.

During the campaign both sides spent a tremendous amount of money on television commercials. The Indians argued that they were being opposed by rich casino operators in Las Vegas who feared competition—a sweeping accusation made all the more effective by the fact that it was absolutely true. Proposition 1A passed by a huge majority. With the Indians now preparing to open full-blown casinos in California, Steve asked that I meet with as many of the tribes as possible to see if there was a possibility of operating their casino projects jointly with them. Actually, he put it to me this way: "Skip, we have to become part of the If-You-Can't-Beat-'Em-Join-'Em Tribe and if they say they only want to do business with Indians just tell them you're a 'Nava-jew!'"

This was much easier said than done. For one thing, many of the tribes already had made deals with other companies before we decided this is what we should do. For another thing, most of the California Indians were extremely mad at us, because they knew we were the ones that had helped finance the opposition to their casino propositions.

Nevertheless I saddled up and headed west. During 1999 Victor, Bruce and I visited about fifty of the one hundred federally recognized tribes in California. The other fifty tribes are in such dreadful locations that they could never open casinos. They are up on mountaintops and in such out-of-the-way places that that they are literally past the end of the road.

My first memorable stop was Palm Springs, where I met with Richard Milanovich, chairman of the Agua Caliente Tribe. Agua Caliente is Spanish for "hot water," and that's exactly what I was in when I showed up at the tribal offices.

The Agua Calientes were acutely aware that Mirage Resorts was one of their prime opponents to Proposition 5. Chairman

Milanovich said the only way we could even enter into a conversation would be if the tribal council approved the discussions, and he ushered me into a large conference room where there were six Indians sitting up on a makeshift stage. It looked like a poor man's nightmare version of "The People's Court."

The council's three female members, solidly-built and scowling, were particularly incensed. They were just waiting for an opportunity to vent, and I was the perfect target. They spent about a half hour berating me and blaming me for all the bad things that had happened to the Indians since Columbus had landed. I was starting to feel a lot like I did in Atlantic City, so I apologized for Chris, then decided to pick up and move on to the next tribe, farther down I-10 in the Coachella Valley.

That was where I made my pitch to the Soboba Tribe, headed up by its chairman Bobby Selgado. Chairman Selgado kept a baseball bat—complete with bloodstains and hair on the sweet spot—in his office, the message being that he was in the habit of taking batting practice on tribal opponents' heads. Once we got past the diatribe concerning our company's apparent attempt to stop their progress, he actually was quite reasonable. The only problem was that their reservation was in such a remote area that there was no way people would drive 15 miles through winding two-lane roads to reach it.

My most productive sales call was even farther down I-10, in Indio. That's where I met with Mark Nichols, the non-Indian CEO of the Cabazon tribe. The Cabazons had an existing casino known as Fantasy Springs. They had big plans for it, but as the saying goes, they had "champagne taste on a beer-drinker's budget." Their site was directly on I-10, and I believed that we could create something pretty special on their property. During the next several weeks I had about a dozen meetings with Nichols, and we forged an agreement that enabled Mirage to be the tribe's partner in what certainly would become a major resort hotel and casino.

During our discussions Nichols always said that the tribe's chairman need not be actively involved in our discussions but would have to be taken on a trip to Las Vegas at some point to see our hotel-casinos for himself. Then, Nichols said, he would undoubtedly bless our agreement.

A date was set up and I took the company's DC-9, the flagship of the Mirage fleet, to Thermal Airport in Indio. There I picked up not only Mark Nichols and the tribe's chairman but also six members of the Cabazon tribal council. We flew to Las Vegas to book them into the Bellagio, meet with Steve Wynn and show them everything we had created. We arranged to have dinner in a private area of Prime, one of the Bellagio's gourmet restaurants. Steve and Elaine Wynn were there, as were my colleagues Victor Cruse, Elizabeth Blau (the woman responsible for the company's restaurant development and daughter of my best friends, Jeffrey and Lynn Blau), and all the tribal members.

From the get-go it was pretty obvious that the chairman was less than the perfect dinner guest. At first he was monosyllabic; after imbibing several tongue-loosening beverages, however, he opened up.

Elaine Wynn, a gracious host, asked the chairman if he had been to Las Vegas before. His response: "Yeah. In fact, I used to go to the Horseshoe downtown, before they started filling it up with Chinks." All the color drained from Elaine's face. He followed that slur with, "Well, I guess they're better than Japs."

Quickly changing the subject, the name of General Colin Powell came up in the conversation. The chairman responded, "Oh yeah. He's what I call one of those *shiny* black guys. You know, like Michael Jordan and Bill Cosby." With that Victor Cruse, my right-hand man whom you might recall happens to be African American, looked like he was going to jump across the table and strangle this guy. I dug my fingers into Victor's thigh and managed to restrain him.

Thankfully, the dinner was soon complete and we had made arrangements for the tribal leaders to attend the "O" show, performed by Cirque du Soleil in our showroom. As we were leaving the restaurant Mark Nichols said, "I told you that this could be a little uncomfortable." A *little*?

"The good news," he said quickly, "is now that we've gotten this out of the way, you'll never have to see or deal with him again."

The next morning I flew with the tribe back to Palm Springs. Steve Wynn asked where I was headed, and when I told him he said, "Great. I'll join you on the trip back there."

Steve sat in the front of the plane with some of the tribal members while I sat in the back with Victor, Mark Nichols and the tribe's chairman. While Steve was regaling his audience with stories, the chairman said to me, "I'm glad I got to meet Steve Wynn. I can tell he's tough, and I like that. That's why Hitler was a great man."

What? I responded angrily, "Yeah. That's true. That's why Custer was a great man."

The chairman glared at me with narrowed eyes and said, "*General* Custer?"

I said, "*Adolf* Hitler?"

Just then the plane touched down, and when we came to a stop the chairman stormed off the plane. Steve Wynn worked his way to the back of the DC-9 and asked where the chairman had gone.

I explained what had happened and Steve was incredulous. I said, "We won't be seeing these Indians again. We can't do business with them."

My cell phone rang. It was Mark Nichols. He said, "Oh, my God! I am so sorry! I know you're Jewish and I can only imagine what you're thinking, but I need you to know that he meant nothing by that remark. He truly doesn't know better. Please give me a chance to make this right."

The next day I got a phone call at the Mirage offices. It was Nichols explaining that he had sat with the chairman and explained to him in great detail how his remarks were beyond offensive. Nichols said the chairman was horrified to think that what he had said was so upsetting to me, and asked if I could please come over to the tribal offices just one more time so that he could apologize for his remarks.

Later that week I made another trip to the reservation. It was the day before Christmas. I was walking behind Nichols when he passed the open door to the chairman's office. When he saw Mark he yelled out, "Merry Christmas!" Then he spotted me and followed with, "And a Happy Hannukah to you!"

———

Back in Atlantic City, minor skirmishes were still going on. Trump didn't quit—I don't think "surrender" is in his vocabulary—but his attacks didn't have the same flare as his previous maneuvers. One of the odder developments in 1999 came in a lawsuit Mirage filed against Trump. It claimed that Donald, working with a couple of Mirage employees, had stolen trade secrets and high roller lists. It was an echo of the Obie affair, and if things like this hadn't been going on since the day we got to Atlantic City, I would have paid it more notice. It was just the latest in a bizarre series of events and more fuel for the Trump-Wynn feud that would seemingly never end.

But everything eventually comes to a close, and the conclusion of this episode in my life was much closer than I had thought. The groundbreaking of the tunnel was a wonderful celebration, but it was meant as a precursor to the ribbon cutting at Le Jardin. That day would never come. After all the lawsuits, lobbying and name-calling, the battle between Wynn and Trump would be decided by a third party, someone who had yet to enter the fight.

CHAPTER 13

The End,
The Beginning

THE FEUD that divided Steve Wynn and Donald Trump throughout the 90s had as much to do with their similarities as their differences. Both men understand the impact a cult of personality has on the bottom line. They live very much in the public eye and use the aspect of celebrity to their advantage. In this respect, they are in stark contrast to an investor like Kirk Kerkorian. Kerkorian generally avoids interviews and would never appear in a commercial, much less a TV show. While his approach is quite different from that of his younger rivals, there is no debating Kerkorian's success. He routinely makes an appearance in the upper echelon of the Forbes 400.

A pilot like fellow Las Vegas pioneer Howard Hughes, Kerkorian has a legendary reputation that extends through several industries from auto manufacturing to film. However, he is best known as the "father of the mega-resort"; originating the impossibly large desert palaces that Steve Wynn had subsequently taken to a new level of sophistication.

Steve and Kirk had great respect for one another, and though they were competing against each other on the Strip, the relationship had always been professional and unmarked by the sort of mudslinging that was a part of the daily routine in New Jersey. While Mirage was locking horns with Trump, MGM Grand was also exploring the possibility of building a casino in Atlantic City. However, by 2000 they had yet to make significant inroads.

We were experiencing our own delays. Though we were close to getting started on the Borgata, the joint venture with Boyd Gaming, Steve still hadn't finalized the design or conclusively settled on the name for the Le Jardin project. The Bellagio was doing tremendous business, but some analysts were apprehensive about the $300 million that had gone into the resort's collection of Impressionist paintings. Added to their concern was the Beau Rivage resort in Biloxi, Mississippi, which had opened less than a year before. Although it was profitable from day one, Beau Rivage met, but did not wildly exceed expectations, as had been the case with each of the company's previous openings. It was assumed that Mirage would deliver a knockout every single time, and in this case we had produced a workmanlike victory. Wall Street was expecting more, and for the first time, the company's stock took a significant hit.

In February 2000, Mirage stock was trading at around eleven dollars a share, less than half the price it was selling for the previous year. Steve asked me if he thought we could add some cash to the company by selling the fifty-acre hole in the H-Tract development plan that Circus Circus had left by pulling out of the deal. I suggested that a logical buyer would be MGM Grand Inc., since Kerkorian's giant Las Vegas-based company had been trying to enter the Atlantic City market for years but couldn't come up with a desirable site.

"Good idea," said Steve.

So he called Kirk Kerkorian and pitched him on building an

MGM Grand resort on the H-Tract. The triumvirate of Le Jardin, the Borgata and an MGM project would radically transform Atlantic City and claim a large chunk of the East Coast gaming market.

"That's interesting," said Kerkorian. "Let me talk to the boys." The boys being MGM Grand CEO Terry Lanni and his other senior executives. "I'll check with them and get back to you."

Kerkorian had a much bigger acquisition in mind. He called Steve back and said, "I think your company is undervalued."

"So do I," said Steve.

Kerkorian continued, "We think it would be smart for us to put these companies together." This was not a casual brainstorming type idea, it was a polite way of saying that Mirage wasn't going to get a partner, but rather a buyer. Kerkorian went on, "In the morning you're going to be getting a letter."

The letter he was referring to was the proverbial "bear hug" letter. A bear hug is an unsolicited bid to a board of directors, an offer they technically can, but shouldn't refuse. There was no "for sale sign" on Mirage, but MGM was after it anyway. Our company was officially "in play."

What happened next is the subject of much misunderstanding and disinformation. When I spoke with Steve, he said, "My gut reaction is we have to fight this." It was a perfectly understandable feeling. After all, he had taken over a struggling Las Vegas hotel and created a company that was the industry standard. Many firms could be run by any competent businessman, but there are exceptions. Apple would not be Apple without Steve Jobs and Mirage would not have been Mirage were it not for Steve Wynn. He didn't want his projects—the hotels he had poured so much time and creativity into—to be subsumed by MGM Grand.

However, after the initial wave of emotion passed, Steve began to see the other side and he realized the opportunity that had been made available to him had some appealing aspects. Any talk that he "lost" Mirage or that Kirk Kerkorian "took" or even "stole" it from him is simply wrong. With Nevada's casino licensing regulations and certain poison-pill provisions in Mirage's corporate bylaws, we could have kept Mirage out of anyone else's hands for years. If Steve wanted to fight, it was a battle he would have won. But the truth was that Steve was and is a compulsively honest businessman. He felt that his highest responsibility was to provide the maximum value for his shareholders, and if that involved selling out to somebody else, so be it. While Mirage Resorts Inc. may have been synonymous with Steve Wynn, it was a public company, and Steve was not going to shirk from his fiduciary duties. Still, if there were to be a sale, Steve was going to make sure we got a good price.

The dance began. MGM offered $17 a share. Mirage responded by calling the initial offer "inadequate." The major players on both sides were master bargainers and within a little more than a week we agreed upon $21 a share as a fair sum. That was nearly twice Mirage's pre-takeover share price. To determine the company's value, MGM calculated the worth of each of our hotels: the Golden Nugget in downtown Las Vegas, the Golden Nugget in Laughlin, the Mirage, Treasure Island, the Bellagio, a half interest in the Monte Carlo Hotel in Las Vegas, and the Beau Rivage in Biloxi. I was particularly proud that MGM valued Mirage's interest in the H-Tract, which we had obtained for virtually nothing, at close to $400 million. When it was all said and done, MGM ended up buying Mirage Resorts for $6.4 billion. The new company, MGM Mirage, now owned the lion's share of the rooms in Las Vegas, a total it added to several years later when it acquired the Mandalay Resort Group—the company formerly known as Circus Circus.

———

The merger had come out of nowhere and was completed with such expediency that I went through an assortment of different emotions in only a few days. Surprise turned into sadness, which morphed into excitement and ended up as dizzying combination of both hope and regret. Though my feelings were in constant flux, I didn't have time to let them settle before taking action. For five years I had been accustomed to a distorted calendar; things that should have taken days stretched out over months. Now the equation was reversed, and there was precious little time to wrap up the project's loose ends.

I had the unenviable task of telling our New Jersey supporters that we were selling the company. I went to see Christie Todd Whitman at her field offices in Newark. Over the years I have had countless meetings with governors, mayors, and other high-ranking officials, and all those appointments had one thing in common: the presence of at least one aide. Politicians like to be surrounded by their assistants, they can't afford having someone call foul with no one there to counter the allegation. However, as I sat down to speak with Whitman one last time, there was curiously no one else in the room. It felt disturbingly calm.

Weicker and Roland had been vague allies even in the best of times, but Whitman's support was unwavering. Our disagreement on July 4, 1996, had derived from misunderstanding involving Jack Innis, not political maneuvering. She had always been a proponent of our development of the H-Tract and her commitment was invaluable to the project. I wasn't happy to inform her that her partner in this struggle was about to be sold. I explained to her that we hadn't planned on the sale—the proposal truly came out of nowhere—but as a public company, our primary obligation was to the shareholders.

The governor clasped her hands together and said, "Skip, after all this drama, after all these battles, I just can't believe this."

I knew how she felt. We had won, we had beaten back every attack, defeated all the lawsuits, and now we weren't going to reap the rewards of our labor. I assured her that I had spoken with the people at MGM and that they had every intention of building a casino in Atlantic City.

I said, "Governor, one day you and I are going to take a ride through the tunnel to the H-Tract and you're going to see that every prediction Steve Wynn made has come true."

She just smiled at me and replied, "If you say so."

———

With Mirage gone, so was New City Development. Also, in all probability, would be the giant resort-casino I'd been working on for almost five years. Regardless of what MGM may have wanted to do, they would have their hands full just taking control of all the existing Mirage properties, so it was unlikely that any new projects, aside from the Borgata, would be built any time soon. I'd make plenty of money from the sale of my stock and options with the MGM takeover—but my whole effort hadn't been about the money. A true developer lives to develop; seeing a world-class resort rise from the barren H-Tract was the dream that had kept me going all those long days and sleepless nights. It was also why my fine team of New City associates had hung in there right alongside me. Though our tasks had been to handle the acquisition of the land, gain the support of the politicians and community, and ensure that all the conditions for development were in order— goals we had accomplished on every level—realizing that none of us would be able to point with pride to what we had helped build left me with a feeling of disappointment.

———

However, there was no time to waste pondering what might have been. Instead, it was time to turn our attentions to what was next. Kerkorian, like Steve, believed that competition was good for the industry as a whole; and one of the key aspects of the MGM-Mirage deal was that it didn't feature a non-competitive clause. Steve Wynn might have been without his company, but he was not without resources. Steve still had his Midas touch, his strong reputation was firmly intact, and after the merger, he had considerable capital to start another project. So he got right back on the horse. Actually, he never got off it. Even while the logistics of the takeover were being worked out, Steve, Frank Dragone—the producer who had masterminded Cirque du Soleil—and I took a trip down Las Vegas Blvd., a stone's throw from the Mirage, to the site of the Desert Inn. Steve bought the land from Barry Sternlicht of Starwood (for a fraction of what it's currently worth), imploded the hotel, and once again attracted scores of investors eager to climb on his bandwagon. In 2002, he began building Wynn Las Vegas. It opened to rave reviews in 2005. Despite what you may have heard or read, getting "revenge" on MGM or Kirk Kerkorian had nothing to do with it. It was all about his passion for creating another ultra-luxurious masterpiece, and Wynn Las Vegas set a new standard for resorts worldwide.

Perfectionists are never satisfied. I was at a Tiger Woods event where a reporter asked the golfer—probably the greatest golfer that ever lived—why he was tinkering with his swing. After all, why mess with success? Tiger responded by saying, "In golf, you're always getting better or getting worse. You don't stay the same." It's a sentiment that applies to many pursuits, certainly the casino industry. It doesn't matter how spectacular the last venture was, there's always something to correct. Be it a small detail, like ensuring elevators go all the way to the spa so guests don't have to walk through the lobby in their bathrobes, or a more significant change, like allowing natural sunlight in a casino, Steve is constantly searching for ways to one-up himself. His latest project is Encore, next door to Wynn Las Vegas, and he opened a huge resort in Macau, just off the coast of Hong Kong, as well. The man who had launched the wave of themed casinos now built hotels with uncomplicated elegance, and the Wynn brand is the strongest in the business. I've enjoyed watching my close friend get all the plaudits and attention he deserves. Talk about reinventing yourself.

Though the Wynn Las Vegas was a tempting opportunity, I was not so eager to get right back in the game, certainly not on the scale of what Steve had planned. I had been working on some Indian casino deals in California and was ready to relocate to Los Angeles and focus on my own company.

Moving to California would have meant being able to spend time with my sister, Janet Cohen. She was a world-class contract bridge player and, in fact, the youngest Life Master in the game's history, women's national champion, captain of the U.S. team in the World Bridge Championship, and the next year would have become the first woman in history to head the 160,000 member American Contract Bridge League. Unfortunately, before I relocated to L.A. Janey passed away at age sixty-two due to lung cancer. She wasn't a smoker, but all that time spent in smoke-filled card rooms finally caught up with her.

———

I know nature hates a vacuum, and so do business and politics. Still, to see the world move on and fill the hole created by our departure from Atlantic City was truly amazing. It all seemed to happen so quickly. As expected, Kirk Kerkorian and Terry Lanni decided that MGM had too much on its plate to go ahead with building a major project on the H-Tract. As soon as that announcement was made, Donald Trump underwent a miraculous change of heart. The man who had fought us so passionately decided that the Brigantine Connector, after all was said and done, *wasn't* a shameless waste of public money, an egregious form of corporate welfare, or an environmental catastrophe waiting to happen. It was a project that would improve Atlantic City. A little bit of politicking even got a nice little off-ramp—aimed straight at Trump Marina Casino—added to the Connector's master plan. Trump's newly reacquired billboards invited East Coast gaming enthusiasts to take advantage of the Brigantine Connector and come on down to Atlantic City. The tunnel's primary antagonist ended up its greatest beneficiary.

———

Just before I decided to pack up and head west full-time, I got an invitation from Ed Gordon, a tremendously successful New York real estate broker. Ed had a Rees Jones-designed golf course on his property, Three Ponds Farm in Bridgehampton, New York, and he invited me to join. Only one other new member was to be inducted with me: Donald Trump. The wounds from the War at the Shore were still fresh and here I was, expected to spend a weekend with the man who had been battling my company for five years. Ed was neither naïve as to what had gone on between Mirage and Trump, nor was he trying to stir up mischief. He simply believed that Donald and I had a lot in common and Ed was determined to convince us as well.

When we got to Ed's place, Donald and I stared each other down as if we were ready to draw pistols. It was, as expected, awkward. Ed's wife Cheryl said that the women (Edie, Cheryl and Donald's then-girlfriend and now wife Melania) were going to town. That would leave Donald and me free to hit the course and determine who was the better golfer.

I was prepared for one of those experiences filled with sublimated anger, but we started playing and immediately developed a rapport. Whatever Donald may have said about Steve—regardless of how personal the comments seemed—it really was all about business. And as for the retorts Mirage had thrown his way, Donald easily shrugged them off. A lot of people will say "It's in the past, I'm over it," but on the inside, it's eating them up. Not Donald. He truly doesn't take anything personally. The whole feud had been a game to him and now that it was over, he was ready to move on. Though I had struggled against him for five years, my contact had been primarily with his representatives and allies. Now that I finally got a chance to get to know him personally, I discovered that he was a great guy. We developed a close friendship that would eventually lead to a professional relationship. I've worked with him on projects and in these last seven years, we've never discussed what went on in New Jersey.

Over time, the feud between Donald and Steve dissolved into mutual compliments. The Mirage suit was dropped, there were no local politics to argue over, and both men were doing incredibly well. In early 2008, the Trump International Hotel Las Vegas, which doesn't feature a casino, opened up right across the street from the Wynn Las Vegas. After all the chaos that consumed Atlantic City for five years, Steve Wynn and Donald Trump end up as neighbors in Las Vegas.

———

Arthur Goldberg was hospitalized in September 2000. He died of cancer on October 19. He was a shrewd, tough-as-nails businessman—and I doubt I shall see a competitor of his zeal and resourcefulness again.

Bill Gormley recently retired. I attended a dinner honoring his 29 years of service to the state of New Jersey and was greeted by all the old faces I hadn't seen in over a decade: Jim Kennedy, Jim Weinstein, Jim Crawford, James Whelan, Lori Strobel (née Campor). It was like a high school reunion, a gathering of people whom I saw every day for several years before they instantly disappeared from my life. We reminisced and caught up; it was remarkable to see how much had changed, but also, how so many things had stayed the same.

Lorenzo T. Langford, the city councilman who had strongly opposed our efforts to build the Connector, ran against the honorable three-term Atlantic City Mayor James Whelan in the 2001 municipal election—and believe it or not, won. Langford was soundly defeated after only one term as mayor. His successor, Bob Levy, was off to a promising start, until he vanished seemingly into thin air. The disappearing mayor surfaced a month later and resigned his post. In November 2008, Langford became mayor again. Only in Atlantic City.

As for Jim Whelan, after spending his out-of-office years happily working in the Atlantic City school system teaching fourth, fifth and sixth graders how to swim, he returned to politics and became a member of the State Assembly. He is currently in the new Jersey State Senate.

Christie Whitman eventually left her post as New Jersey governor in 2001 to head the Environmental Protection Agency in the Bush administration. She quit that job in 2003—at least partly, they say, because environmental protection wasn't exactly the Bush administration's highest priority. Harriet Derman, Whitman's formidable former chief of staff, is now a judge of the New Jersey State Superior Court. As time heals all wounds, we've gone on to become friends. But I still feel sorry for the lawyers who have to plead their cases before her.

When two companies decide to hunker down and give each other hell, the usual result is a battle nobody wins. The War at the Shore was a rare case of a fight that ended not in the destruction of both sides, but actually a triumph for all involved. I had turned a dump into a $400 million piece of land, and Donald Trump, through attrition, had succeeded in keeping his biggest rival out of his backyard. When you really think about it, that's all Donald was trying to accomplish in the first place. He will fight to the death and at the end of the day, he's actually a brilliant guy who usually winds up with what he wants. In this case, he got even more than he asked for; after all, his casino was the one to reap the rewards of the tunnel. So those who may see Donald Trump as the loser in all of this just don't get it ... nor HIM.

But by far the most amazing consequences of my work in Atlantic City was the way in which the Brigantine Connector revitalized the city's economy and gaming industry.

When MGM bought us out it had absolutely no effect on the fate of the Brigantine Connector. It was completed and opened, on time and under budget, just as Carl Petrillo had promised me. Traffic flow in Atlantic City improved immediately, and the community that the activists said we'd destroy actually benefited greatly from new parklands, less noise and pollution, and a community center we'd funded.

In the meantime MGM, not one to throw in a winning hand, enthusiastically continued the H-Tract joint venture that Mirage had previously formed with Boyd Gaming. The result was the extremely successful Borgata Hotel & Spa, the first new hotel-casino to be built in Atlantic City in thirteen years. When the $1.1 billion resort opened in July 2002, it was a lot like what Mirage had envisioned way back in 1996; an infusion of Las Vegas style and glamour into tired old Atlantic City. Most of the casinos in Atlantic City don't look much more sophisticated than the hotels in Monopoly.

They're box-like structures with drab facades, the names written in a font more commonly found on an auto body shop. From the outside, the Borgata has the golden sheen of the Mandalay Bay and the inside is pure Bellagio. From the glass tentacle Chihuly sculptures to the elegant columns in the corridors to the marble that surrounds the casino (as opposed to the more commonly found wall-to-wall carpeting), it resembles a small Wynn casino and is the only place in New Jersey that could make you feel like you were in Nevada.

Not surprisingly, the Borgata immediately became the highest-grossing and most profitable gaming property in Atlantic City history. It retains that title, even though many of the other hotels in town, particularly Harrah's, have tried to match it with major improvements of their own. The Borgata has the highest return on investment for any non-Indian casino in America. It has become so successful that they just completed an 800-room expansion. As for the rest of the H-Tract (now commonly referred to by the more polished and appropriate moniker Renaissance Point), MGM-Mirage will one day get around to building on it. CityCenter East, a companion to the company's project in Las Vegas, is a massive development estimated to cost over $5 billion.

Not long ago, the developer Herb Simon and I had lunch in Beverly Hills with Terry Lanni. In regard to the unbridled success of the Borgata, Terry said, "Borgata has exceeded everyone's expectations. It's hugely profitable. One thing's for sure: It wouldn't be there if not for the *amazing* job you did."

Amazing. That's not a bad word for the whole experience.

Epilogue

IF YOU'RE LUCKY, you'll have a moment someday when your life winds out into full telescopic view and with a backward glance you can see precisely how far you've come. For me, that moment came on February 12, 2005, on the night of my sixtieth birthday party.

Friends from many chapters of my life gathered at our home in Beverly Hills. After cocktails we had a fabulous lobster dinner. Before dessert came several toasts and tributes.

Scott, my elder son, is not entirely comfortable speaking in front of a crowd, but he was great. "Dad never let a week go by when he didn't tell me how much he loves me or how proud he is of me," he said. "Dad, those words never get tiring, and the feeling's mutual. You never let me down in any way, and you lifted me up when I thought the day would never end. Watching my dad be a father to Annabella is like having déjà vu. Annabelle, you are very lucky."

Jon, my younger son, could do stand-up for a living, but after a few jokes, he got sentimental as well, "You're the greatest father. I love you so much."

Even Annie got up to speak and proved herself as much of a comedian as Jon. "I've come to learn that everyone loves my dad, even though he has his flaws," she said. "But the important thing is he makes everyone laugh. And it's great to know I have a dad that everyone adores. I love you, and happy birthday."

I have to tell you, it was pretty overwhelming to have your kids so openly express their love. It was one of the proudest, most satisfying and most memorable moments of my life.

Steve Wynn, beside whom I'd waged so many memorable battles, stepped up to say a few words. The man that *Time* would name one of the one hundred most influential Americans just a few months later cleared his throat. The crowd quieted.

"Sixty is a big number for a guy," he began. "It's that moment when you know for sure that you never again will be referred to as 'The Kid.' So I thought it might be worth mentioning something that I had the privilege of watching first-hand."

He was referring to the War at the Shore and he went on to recount our quest to build a mega-resort in New Jersey. "The established hotels in Atlantic City were against it, because it would have marked a shift in the center of gravity in the city from the Boardwalk to the marina. The principal players were very influential people, the Bally and Hilton corporations, Arthur Goldberg and Donald Trump. They took extreme exception to the fact that we were going to route all the traffic from the Atlantic City Expressway onto our property and away from the Boardwalk."

Steve pointed out that "Trump and Goldberg represented 85% of the investment in the community," and that they vowed our plan would succeed "'over their dead bodies.' They hired every lobbyist and influential person in the state of New Jersey to stop this from happening. We, on the other hand, had only one person. One person was in charge of: A) Getting a hundred and fifty acres free; B) getting a tunnel built by the state of New Jersey for a mile and a half; C) since this was once a dump site, getting it cleaned up with state and federal money. All of this, as I say, was going to be over Donald Trump's and Arthur Goldberg's dead bodies.

"So on one side were literally fifteen to twenty lobbying firms, and umpteen millions of dollars per year in contributions. And on the other side was...Bronson. This is a guy from Hartford, Connecticut, who told me, 'Look, you're busy with the Bellagio, I'll take care of this.' I said, 'You will, Skip? You think you'll be able to do this? All these guys that don't want to do it? It's gonna be World War III.' And he said, 'Just let me do it. I'll handle it.'

"I got to watch one man from Hartford, Connecticut, go to New Jersey three to four days a week, and personally charm, persuade and convince everybody in that state that what he was proposing was the right thing to do, and that what the other guys were proposing was just pure selfishness, that they didn't know what they were talking about, but that he, from Connecticut, knew what he was talking about. It was an incredible demonstration of a man's ability not just to influence others, but to use persuasive, intelligent arguments of the highest level involving politics, money, and economics.

"There was a statement made by one of the newscasters who said, 'If it was a fight, they would have stopped it.' The score was 12-0. It wasn't even close. We got the property for nothing, we got the tunnel, we got a law passed that said if anybody fixes up a dump site they'll get a tax credit. It was one of the most masterful performances that I've seen in my thirty-five years in business."

———

States desperate for revenue and a means of assuaging the problem that isn't as easy politically as it is logically; no, I'm not talking about a new casino, I'm talking about Internet gambling.

A lot of people are surprised to hear that online poker isn't legal. There wasn't significant legislation against it until 2006, and it took the federal government almost five more years to crack down on all the illegal offshore operators. Now the dust is starting to clear, and the push for legalization is gaining momentum every day.

While I continue to work in development, I've set my sites on the last frontier of gaming. As Chairman and Founder of U.S. Digital Gaming, a company that provides an end-to-end solution for legalized online gambling, I've stepped into a new arena—and faced a lot of the old challenges. Of course, now it's not running what amounts to a political campaign in a single state, but rather, various campaigns across the country. One week California seems poised to be the first state to give the green light, the next week, Iowa. I don't know when or will it will happen, but it is inevitable, and when it does come to pass, it will revolutionize the gambling industry.

———

When I return to Connecticut now and then I'm reminded of the unmatched success of the Mohegan Sun and Foxwoods. Every year they vie for the top spot among casinos in terms of profitability (this is due to their exposure to large markets and no competition aside from one another). However, it's a distinction neither would have earned were it not for the presence of slot machines, and that wouldn't have happened if Mirage hadn't attempted to build a casino in Connecticut. In Atlantic City, the Borgata has dominated its competition, but without the Brigantine Connector, it would have been merely a blueprint.

Every time I drive that two-mile stretch, my mind flashes back to that fateful day when the police officer who I thought was there to preserve order declared, "Before they put a brick in front of my house, I will throw a brick at them!" His name was Jeffree Fauntleroy, and he was vice president of the Westside Homeowners Protective Association.

Fauntleroy's comments were all that was needed to push an excited crowd over the edge. I feared that if I didn't leave at that moment, the consequences might be dire. With my heart ready to bust out of my chest and my palms moist to the point where I struggled to hold the microphone, I made a beeline for the door. I didn't look behind me, but I could hear the frustrated rage at my back. I jumped in my car, which, unintentionally but quite fortuitously, was parked right by the exit.

Once inside, I turned to Victor and he said to me with a sadness deepened by understanding, "There are wounds that have nothing to *do* with us and everything to do with taking it *out* on us."

I hope those wounds have started to heal, but as I follow the drama of New Jersey politics from a safer distance, it appears little has changed the way business is done. The War at the Shore may be over, but there's always a battle brewing in Atlantic City.

Notes

Chapter 5

1. Chris Smith, "Clash of the Titans," *The New Yorker*, 2/16/98.
2. Smith.
3. Quoted in *Philadelphia Inquirer*, 9/7/95.

Chapter 6

1. Quoted in *The Press of Atlantic City*, 11/14/95.
2. Quoted in *The Press of Atlantic City*, 1/24/96
3. Quoted in *The Star-Ledger* (Newark, NJ), 1/24/96.

Chapter 7

1. Quoted in *The Press of Atlantic City*, 3/12/96.
2. Quoted in *The Press of Atlantic City*, 3/21/96.
3. Quoted in *The Press of Atlantic City*, 3/29/96.

Chapter 9

1. *The Press of Atlantic City*, 9/20/96.
2. Quoted in *The Press of Atlantic City*, 9/22/96.
3. Quoted in *The Press of Atlantic City*, 3/21/97.
4. Quoted in *The Press of Atlantic City*, 3/28/97.
5. Quoted in *The Press of Atlantic City*, 6/1/97.

Chapter 11

1. Quoted in *The Press of Atlantic City*, 7/1/97.
2. *The Press of Atlantic City*, 1/21/98.